Topics in Communication Theory

McGraw-Hill Monographs in Modern Engineering Science

Richard E. Bellman and Robert Kalaba, Editors

Angelo and Papoulis *Pole-Zero Patterns in the Analysis and Design of Low-order Systems*

Lorens *Flowgraphs: For the Modeling and Analysis of Linear Systems*

Middleton *Topics in Communication Theory*

Moore *Wave and Diffusion Analogies*

Pfeiffer *Sets, Events, and Switching*

Topics in Communication Theory

David Middleton

Consulting Physicist
and
Adjunct Professor of Communication Theory and Applied Physics at Rensselaer Polytechnic Institute

McGraw-Hill Book Company

New York St. Louis San Francisco Toronto London

TOPICS IN COMMUNICATION THEORY

Library of Congress Catalog Card Number 64-25001

To George Middleton
and Fola La Follette

Preface

"Was Du ererbt von deinen Vätern hast Erwirb es, um es zu besitzen."

Faust, I.

The purpose of this monograph is to provide an introductory treatment of several basic problems that commonly occur in communication theory. For the most part the emphasis is on formulation and method, rather than on detailed analysis and specialized results, which are considered elsewhere.[1,2] The topics examined here are the detection of signals in noise, their extraction from noise, and the interpretation of optimum system structure for these purposes, from the unifying viewpoint of statistical decision theory. Chapter 1 presents the required formulation; Chapters 2 and 3 are devoted principally to optimum signal detection and extraction, respectively, while Chapter 4 concentrates on the corresponding system realizations. Chapter 5 completes the discussion with a critique of the general approach and mention of some of the current areas of application and future development. Several examples demonstrate the general methods used, and various extensions are included for illustration. An Appendix contains a number of mathematical results needed in the examples.

This short monograph is intended for the technically

qualified nonspecialist and for interested students at the upper division levels. It may also serve as an introduction to the author's earlier and more comprehensive treatment (part IV of Ref. 1). An adequate mathematical background on the part of the reader is necessarily assumed; elements of probability theory and statistics, matrices, Fourier transforms, calculus of variations, and the usual apparatus of advanced calculus. A number of new results are included, specifically in Secs. 2.6, 2.7, 3.4, and 3.5, and elements of Chap. 4. These are mainly along the lines of a canonical theory of threshold detection, with applications and extensions to signal extraction as well (Chap. 4), including several specific new results in detection and extraction theory. Spatial limitations, however, preclude a detailed development. Neither is it possible, for similar reasons, to consider many other equally important and interesting topics that legitimately belong to the domain of communication theory—such as coding and information measures, noise theory, sequential methods, signal analysis, and random processes. These are, on the other hand, in the main adequately covered elsewhere (Ref. 1, and the Bibliography that follows Chap. 5). A few selected references at the end of each chapter may serve to orient the reader's further interests.

The author acknowledges with pleasure his debt to Dr. Robert Kalaba for his constructive comments and to Mrs. William Denney for her careful preparation of a not entirely simple manuscript.

David Middleton

1. D. Middleton: "An Introduction to Statistical Communication Theory," McGraw-Hill Book Company, New York, 1960; in particular, part IV.
2. Д. Миддлтон: Введение в Статистическую Теорию Связи, Том 1, 1961; Том 2, 1962, Советское Радио, Москва, С.С.С.Р. (vol. 1, 1961; vol. 2, 1962, Soviet Radio, Moscow, U.S.S.R.).

Contents

Chapter 1

Communication from the Viewpoint of Decision Theory

The communication processes that we shall consider in this monograph are those that involve the transmission of information between a single source and a single receiver. Specifically, "information" is used here in the technical sense of different degrees of certainty and uncertainty, and not necessarily in the broader sense of "information" as meaning. Communication theory is thus regarded basically as a statistical process, where appropriate probabilistic models and methods are required for the solution of problems.

The statistical approach is inevitable, since we are concerned not with the transmission and reception of just one particular "message," but rather with the set, or ensemble, of all possible messages for the purpose at hand. Furthermore, as these necessarily take place in the course of finite (nonzero) periods of time, our ensemble is thus a random process, for the description and treatment of which an extensive mathematical apparatus is now available.[1,2]

Accordingly, communication theory from the analytical viewpoint may be regarded as a theory dealing with certain selected operations on ensembles. Just what these operations, or transformations, are will depend on the purpose of the communication process, the physical environment in which it is embedded, and the physical means by which it is to be realized, namely, the specific means and methods of transmission and reception themselves. Our first task here is to develop these ideas in quantitative form, and our second is to show how they may be applied to such basic communication problems as signal detection, extraction, and the interpretation of optimum system structures for these purposes.

1.1 *Introduction: The Single-link System*

Let us begin by observing that real communication processes are always subject to error, because of interference, or "noise," introduced by the physical environment in which the processes take place. This noise may arise from a variety of causes, man-made or natural, but it nevertheless limits the accuracy of transmission and reception and strongly influences the overall design of the desired communication system. Some systems will perform better than others against noise, and so we are naturally led to look for *optimum* systems for the purpose at hand. In other instances we must be content with *suboptimum* systems, but in all cases it is clearly desirable to know where optimality lies and how close the expected system performance may come to it. While there are often many other more or less serious constraints on system design and operation, such as time, bandwidth, complexity, and cost, it is the unremovable physical noise which sets the fundamental limitation on performance, and in the finite processing time available to us the effects of this noise can never be wholly eliminated.

With the above in mind we may specify the aims of an adequate theory of optimum system performance and design. Such a theory should provide:

1. System structure—the specific operations for optimal transmission and reception
2. Evaluation of performance—quantitative measures of optimum performance for the ensemble of possible "messages"
3. Comparison with other suboptimum systems, for the same purpose and (usually) under the same external conditions of operation

To make these notions more precise, let us consider the basic single-link communication system of the present discussion. It may be compactly described by the relation

$$\{v\} = T_R^{(N)} T_M^{(N)} T_T^{(N)} \{u\} \tag{1.1}$$

where $\{u\}$ represents an ensemble of possible messages at the source, or transmitting end of the link, that result in a set of received messages $\{v\}$ or decisions consequent upon them. The T's are transformations which embody the operations of encoding $(T_T^{(N)})$, the effects $(T_M^{(N)})$ of the channel or medium of propagation through which the "output," or transmitted signals $\{x\} = T_T^{(N)}\{u\}$, are sent, and the operation of the receiver $(T_R^{(N)})$ on the received signals $\{y\} = T_M^{(N)}\{x\} = T_M^{(N)} T_T^{(N)}\{u\}$, to convert them to the desired messages or decisions $\{v\}$. The superscript $^{(N)}$ refers to the possible injection of noise into the system at the

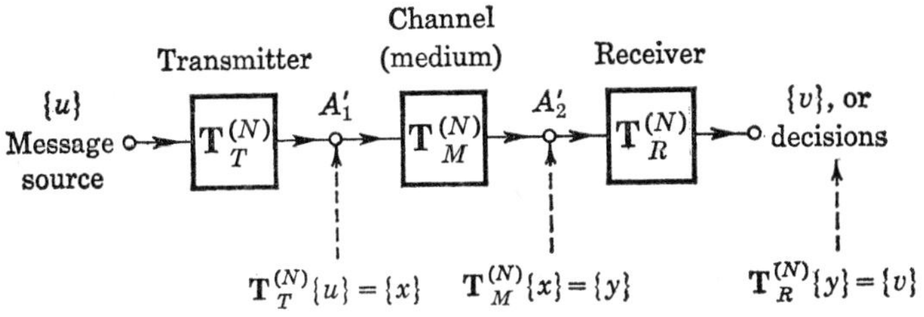

Fig. 1.1 Schema of the single-link communication system of Eq. (1.1).

stage indicated. Thus, $T_R^{(N)}$ indicates that noise is injected at one or more stages in the reception process, and so on for $T_T^{(N)}$, etc. Figure 1.1 illustrates the basic single-link system.

The central aim of a general communication system

$$(T_R^{(N)} T_M^{(N)} T_T^{(N)}\{\quad\})$$

is to render $\{v\}$ acceptably "close" in some specific sense to the original set $\{u\}$. The chief aim of an *optimum* system of this type is to bring the received set $\{v\}$ into closest possible "identity" with the original set $\{v\}$. This is done by suitable choice of the operations $T_R^{(N)}$, $T_T^{(N)}$, or both together. The transformation $T_M^{(N)}$, representing the medium, usually cannot be modified by either transmitter or receiver and constitutes a further and usually serious constraint on system performance. The specific structure and performance of an optimum system will, of course, depend on the criterion of optimality that is selected. Different criteria lead to different systems, in general. Optimum structure and performance also depend on the signals sent and received, on the specific constraints introduced by transmitter, receiver, and channel, and, influencing all these, on the purpose of the communication process itself.

At this point we distinguish two types of communication process: (1) those processes where specific decisions are required, i.e., where a particular "message" $u^{(j)}$ leads to a particular decision consequent upon the corresponding $v^{(j)}$ [cf. Eq. (1.1)], and (2) those operations which do not yield definite decisions. These latter are essentially "mapping" operations, converting the ensemble $\{u\}$ into the ensemble $\{v\}$ according to Eq. (1.1), where input data are supplied and processed to yield output data. The former specifically incorporate the decision-making operations in the processing of the data; the outputs of these systems are definite decisions made in the face of uncertainty which, as noted above, arises because of inherent noise. It is with these, and principally with their optimum forms, that we shall be largely occupied in this book.

Decisions made in the face of uncertainty imply *value judgments* and attendant *errors of decision*. The three chief elements of a *statistical decision theory* are (1) the assignment of quantitative measures, or *costs*, to the possible correct and incorrect decisions that are the outcome of processing the *ensembles* of possible received signals and noise, e.g., $\{y\} = T_M^{(N)}\{x\}$; (2) the introduction of a suitable statistical model to account for the uncertain occurrence of these possibly correct and incorrect decisions; and (3) the choice of a *performance criterion* and the calculation of system performance from it, expressed as some suitable average cost based on (1) and (2).

Our next step, therefore, is to construct a statistical decision theory according to elements (1) to (3) above, to obtain optimum system structure, optimum performance, and comparison with suboptimum systems for similar purposes. The principal areas of application considered here are (1) *signal detection*, in which the basic problem is to determine the presence or absence of a signal in noise, and (2) *signal extraction*, where some information-bearing feature of the signal, or possibly the signal itself, is to be measured, or "extracted," from signals corrupted by noise. Both (1) and (2) require optimization by choice of $T_R^{(N)}$ and sometimes, where possible, by a simultaneous adjustment of $T_R^{(N)}$ and $T_T^{(N)}$, often called *cost coding*.† As we shall see in the next

† Ref. 1, sec. 23.2.

section, the decision-theory approach incorporates within a common formulation the statistical methods developed earlier for more special applications, such as *hypothesis testing*† [signal detection (1)] and *parameter estimation*, including *smoothing* and *prediction* [signal extraction (2)].‡ The approach below is based on decision-theory methods as developed originally by the author and Van Meter[3] for problems of this type.

1.2 Formulation

Let us begin by constructing a model of the communication process in the single-link case according to these general ideas of decision

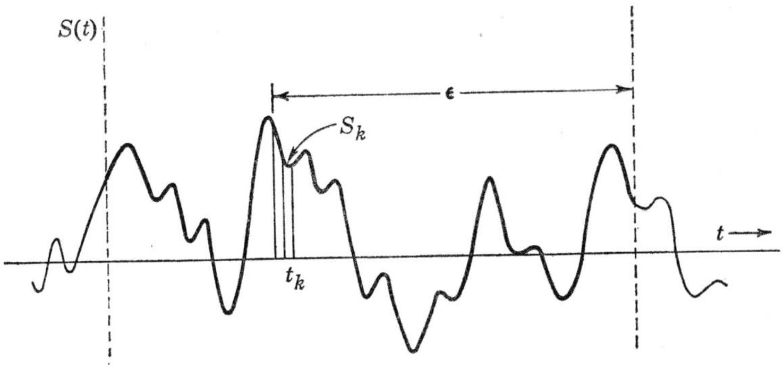

Fig. 1.2 A signal waveform, with sampled values on $(t_0, t_0 + T)$.

theory. First, we introduce abstract signal and data spaces Ω and Γ, respectively, and consider discretely sampled signal and data processes on some finite time interval:

$$\mathbf{S} = [S(t_1), S(t_2), \ldots, S(t_n)] = [S_1, S_2, \ldots, S_n] \qquad (1.2a)$$
$$\mathbf{V} = [V(t_1), V(t_2), \ldots, V(t_n)] = [V_1, V_2, \ldots, V_n] \qquad (1.2b)$$

with $(t_0 \leq t_1 \leq t_2 \leq \cdots \leq t_n \leq T + t_0)$; $\mathbf{S}$ and $\mathbf{V}$ are accordingly n-component vectors in Ω and Γ space. Figure 1.2 shows a typical signal waveform $S(t)$. Figure 1.3 likewise shows a data waveform [here $V(t) = y(t) = \mathbf{T}_M^{(N)}\mathbf{T}_T^{(N)}\{u\}$; cf. Figure 1.1]. The sampling times are t_k, $(k = 1, \ldots, n)$. The times t_λ indicated in Fig. 1.3 refer to instants, usually different from the t_k, at which an estimate of the signal corrupted

† Ref. 1, sec. 18.2-1.
‡ Ref. 1, sec. 18.2-2.

by the accompanying noise may be desired. Accordingly, if $t_\lambda > t_0 + T$, we have an example of *prediction*, while if $t_0 < t_\lambda < t_0 + T$, we have a case of *interpolation;* in general, if $t_\lambda < t_0$ or $t_\lambda > t_0 + T$, we speak of *extrapolation*.

The quantity ϵ in Fig. 1.2 is an *epoch*, which refers the observer's time scale to that on the signal structure; ϵ is usually measured from some distinguishing point on the waveform. The extent to which ϵ is known at the receiver significantly influences the structure and performance of both optimum and suboptimum systems, for both detection and extraction.† When ϵ is known precisely, we have *coherent reception* with coherent sampling.‡ When ϵ is not known and in particular when ϵ

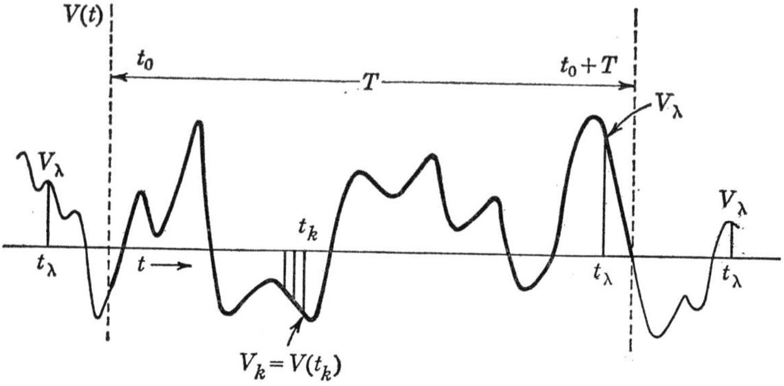

Fig. 1.3 A data waveform, with sampled values in $(t_0, t_0 + T.)$

is uncertain over a time interval that is comparable to, or larger than, an average fluctuation period of the signal, we have *incoherent reception*, with a corresponding sample uncertainty. The sample is the data in $(t_0, t_0 + T)$. We shall see specific examples of this behavior in Chaps. 2 and 4.

The decision situation, in which either a detection or extraction concerning the signal is now required, is depicted in Fig. 1.4. In addition to the data and signal spaces Γ and Ω, we introduce a noise space (N) and a decision space Δ. The vector $\gamma = [\gamma_1, \gamma_2, \ldots, \gamma_m]$ represents a set of m decisions $\gamma_1, \ldots, \gamma_m$ about the signal process $\mathbf{S}$, based on the received data process $\mathbf{V}$. We introduce also the *decision rule*

† Ref. 1, sec. 19.4-3.
‡ *Ibid.*

$\delta(\gamma|\mathbf{V})$, which may be either a probability or a probability density governing the decision γ, based on the data process $\mathbf{V}$.

The quantities $\sigma(\mathbf{S})$ or $\sigma(\boldsymbol{\theta})$, $F_n(\mathbf{V}|\mathbf{S})$, and $\mathbf{W}(\mathbf{N})$ are respectively the distribution densities (d.d.'s) of the following variables: the n-component vector $\mathbf{S}$, or the random parameters $\boldsymbol{\theta}$ of $\mathbf{S}$ when $\mathbf{S} = \mathbf{S}(\boldsymbol{\theta})$ is a deterministic signal process; the data process $\mathbf{V}$, given $\mathbf{S}$, an n-fold joint d.d. also; and the accompanying noise process $\mathbf{N}$, which is combined with $\mathbf{S}$, as indicated by the symbol $\otimes$, to form $\mathbf{V}$, as shown in Fig. 1.4.

The usual combination of signal and noise is additive, so that $\otimes = +$, but it is not uncommon to encounter other situations, where the combination is multiplicative, so that $V = S \times N$ in some sense,

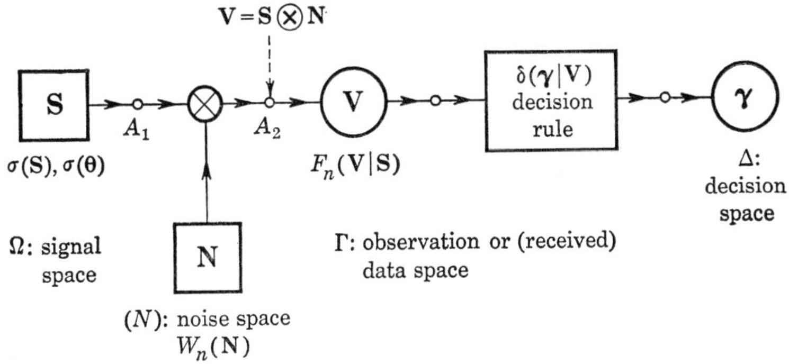

Fig. 1.4 The general decision situation.

or even has additional, additive noise, e.g., $V = S \times N_1 + N_2$ (so that $\otimes = X, +$). Multipath, ground- and sea-clutter, and scatter communications and fading media offer important physical examples of multiplicative combination, which become additive also, when system (receiver) noise is included. In terms of Fig. 1.1, the point A_2 in Fig. 1.4 can usually be taken at A_2' in Fig. 1.1, since in most cases the significant system noise arises physically in the initial, linear stages of practical receivers and so can be regarded as appearing as a source external to $\boldsymbol{T}_R$, i.e., at (N). Similarly, the effect of the medium or channel $\boldsymbol{T}_M^{(N)}$ (between A_1', A_2', Fig. 1.1) is embodied in what happens between A_1, A_2 in the schema of Fig. 1.4. Usually, too, the effects of noise in $\boldsymbol{T}_T^{(N)}$ can be ignored or included in $\mathbf{S}$, its output, so that V above is equivalently

$$V = y = \boldsymbol{T}_M^{(N)}\{S\} \qquad S = \boldsymbol{T}_T^{(N)}\{u\} \tag{1.3}$$

and the decision rule is

$$\delta(\gamma|\mathbf{V}) = T_R\{\mathbf{V}\} = T_R T_M^{(N')}\{\mathbf{S}\} (= T_R^{(N)} T_M^{(N)}\{\mathbf{S}\}) \tag{1.4}$$

(for discrete sampling), where (N') includes receiver noise as well as that of the channel or medium.

The decision rule is the embodiment of receiver structure. When T_R is specified, so also is $\delta(\gamma|\mathbf{V})$ and vice versa. For detection problems, where the system output is of the type "yes" (a signal as well as noise occurs) or "no" (only noise is present), the decisions γ are distinct, discrete points in decision space Δ, and δ itself is a probability ($0 \leq \delta \leq 1$). For signal extraction, however, where the signal S, or its random parameters $\boldsymbol{\theta}$, may take on a continuum of values, δ becomes a probability density ($0 \leq \delta \leq \infty$). In either instance we may distinguish between a *signal class* of one member, and one of two or more members. When we have to deal with a single, nonrandom signal, the input is said (in detection) to belong to a *simple hypothesis class*, and similarly in estimation. On the other hand, a *composite hypothesis* (or signal) *class* contains two or more signal members. It thus asserts the presence at the system's input (i.e., at A_2 in Fig. 1.4, or equivalently at A_2' in Fig. 1.1, as noted above) of an unspecified member of the hypothesis class. In any case, the decision process refers always to the distinguishable subclass and not necessarily to any one signal in it. In this way one takes into account the distribution of possible signals [through $\sigma(\mathbf{S})$ or $\sigma(\boldsymbol{\theta})$; cf. Fig. 1.4], only one of which is to be encountered in a particular situation. We shall see presently how these notions are to be expressed quantitatively.

With the decision situation constructed in terms of the relevant a priori information, as sketched in Fig. 1.4, our next step is to introduce an evaluation function, whereby performance can be evaluated, not only for a particular decision but for the entire set of possible decisions that are the consequences of the ensemble of received data $\mathbf{V}$ and signal process $\mathbf{S}$. Specifically, we seek a suitable statistic by which to describe the system's behavior. Let us accordingly consider a *cost* or *loss function* $\mathfrak{F}(\mathbf{S},\gamma)$, which assigns to each signal (or, in the case of composite signal classes, to each such distinguishable class) and to the decision associated with it a quantitative value judgment, or "cost." The appropriate statistic for evaluating system performance we shall now choose to be the *average cost*, or *average loss* $\mathfrak{L}$, associated with the decision process (1.1):

$$\mathcal{L}(\sigma,\delta) = E_{v,s}\{\mathfrak{F}(\mathbf{S},\gamma(\mathbf{V}))\}$$
$$= \int_\Omega d\mathbf{s}\,\sigma(\mathbf{S}) \left\{\int_\Gamma F_n(\mathbf{V}|\mathbf{S})\, d\mathbf{V} \int_\Delta \delta(\gamma|\mathbf{V})\mathfrak{F}(\mathbf{S},\gamma)\, d\gamma\right\} \tag{1.5a}$$
$$\mathcal{L}(\sigma,\delta) = E_s\{E_v[\mathfrak{F}(\mathbf{S},\gamma(\mathbf{V}))]\} \tag{1.5b}$$

where the expression in braces { } in the second relation of Eq. (1.5*a*) is the *conditional loss* $E_v\{\mathfrak{F}(\mathbf{S},\gamma(\mathbf{V}))\}$. When $\mathbf{S} = \mathbf{S}(\boldsymbol{\theta})$, Eqs. (1.5) are modified to

$$\mathcal{L}(\sigma,\delta) = E_{v,\theta}\{\mathfrak{F}(\mathbf{S},\gamma(\mathbf{V}))\} \quad \text{or} \quad E_{v,\theta}\{\mathfrak{F}(\boldsymbol{\theta},\gamma(\mathbf{V}))\} \tag{1.6}$$

which are not generally equivalent. These forms are often appropriate in estimation problems.

While the number of possible cost functions $\mathfrak{F}$ is extremely large, two cost functions of particular importance in communication-theory applications are (1) the direct or explicit cost function:

$$\mathfrak{F}_1(\mathbf{S},\gamma) = C(\mathbf{S},\gamma) \tag{1.7}$$

where C is independent of the decision rule δ and associates a set of preassigned fixed costs to the various possible decisions γ about $\mathbf{S}$, and (2)

$$\mathfrak{F}_2(\mathbf{S},\gamma) = -\log p(\mathbf{S}|\gamma) \tag{1.8}$$

where p is the posterior probability of $\mathbf{S}$, given γ. Unlike $C(\mathbf{S},\gamma)$, $\mathfrak{F}_2$ depends implicitly on the decision rule δ and consequently cannot be preassigned independently of it. The theory of optimum and sub-optimum systems based on $\mathfrak{F}_2$ is therefore more complex† than that based on $\mathfrak{F}_1$. One reason for selecting $\mathfrak{F}_2$ according to Eq. (1.8) stems from the fact that $-\log p(\mathbf{S}|\gamma)$ is a measure of uncertainty or equivocation in the information-theory sense.‡ Putting Eqs. (1.7) and (1.8) into (1.5) gives us respectively the following average losses:

$$\mathcal{L}_1 \equiv R(\sigma,\delta)$$
$$= \int_\Omega \sigma(\mathbf{S})\, d\mathbf{S} \left\{\int_\Gamma F_n(\mathbf{V}|\mathbf{S})\, d\mathbf{V} \int_\Delta \delta(\gamma|\mathbf{V})C(\mathbf{S},\gamma)\, d\gamma\right\}$$
$$= \text{average cost} \tag{1.9}$$

$$\mathcal{L}_2 \equiv H(\sigma,\delta)$$
$$= -\int_\Omega \sigma(\mathbf{S})\, d\mathbf{S} \left\{\int_\Gamma F_n(\mathbf{V}|\mathbf{S})\, d\mathbf{V} \int_\Delta \delta(\gamma|\mathbf{V}) \log p(\mathbf{S}|\gamma)\, d\gamma\right\}$$
$$= \text{average information loss} \tag{1.10}$$

† Ref. 1, chap. 22.
‡ Ref. 1, secs. 6.2-1 and 22.1-2.

[When $\mathbf{S} = \mathbf{S}(\boldsymbol{\theta})$ one simply replaces $\sigma(\mathbf{S})\,\mathbf{dS}$ by $\sigma(\boldsymbol{\theta})\,\mathbf{d\theta}$ in the above.† We observe again that the decision rule δ is a probability in the case of detection. The integral representation over decision space Δ is in effect a sum over the discrete and distinct points in this abstract space that represent the decisions $\gamma_1, \ldots, \gamma_m$.]

For extraction problems, which are basically measurement operations —"how much" or "what magnitude," as distinct from the typically "yes" or "no" decision of detection—the decision rule δ becomes a probability density; for example,

$$\delta(\boldsymbol{\gamma}|\mathbf{V}) = \delta(\mathbf{S} - \boldsymbol{\gamma}_\sigma(\mathbf{V})) \qquad \text{or} \qquad \delta(\boldsymbol{\theta} - \boldsymbol{\gamma}_\sigma(\mathbf{V})) \tag{1.11}$$

The right-hand members of (1.11) are delta functions,‡ and $\boldsymbol{\gamma}_\sigma(\mathbf{V}) \equiv \boldsymbol{\gamma}_\sigma(\mathbf{S}|\mathbf{V})$, or $\boldsymbol{\gamma}_\sigma(\boldsymbol{\theta}|\mathbf{V})$, is the *estimator* (here of $\mathbf{S}$, or $\boldsymbol{\theta}$) based on the received data $\mathbf{V}$ and subject to the d.d., σ, of $\mathbf{S}$ (or of $\boldsymbol{\theta}$).

Prediction and *smoothing* (e.g., filtering), as well as simple estimation ($t_\lambda = t_k$, $k = 1, \ldots, n$), are easily included in the present formalism. We may write Eq. (1.9) with the help of (1.11) as

$$R(\sigma,\delta) = \int_\Omega \sigma(\mathbf{S},S_\lambda)\,\mathbf{dS}\,dS_\lambda \int_\Gamma F_n(\mathbf{V}|\mathbf{S})C(\mathbf{S},f(S_\lambda);\boldsymbol{\gamma}_\sigma)\,\mathbf{dV} \tag{1.12}$$

with now $\boldsymbol{\gamma}_\sigma = \boldsymbol{\gamma}_\sigma(\mathbf{S}'|\mathbf{V})$, where $\mathbf{S}'$ is the $(n + 1)$-component vector $[\mathbf{S},f(S_\lambda)]$. For example, we may have $f(S_\lambda) = S_\lambda$, which is the predicted value of S at t_λ. Other types of extrapolation may occur: thus $f(S_\lambda) = \dot{S}_\lambda$ is the predicted value of $\dot{S}$ at t_λ, and so on; f, of course, need not be linear, and C can be quite general. The classical prediction theory of Wiener[4] and Kolmogoroff[5] (where f is linear and C is quadratic) is in this way conceptually and operationally incorporated into the decision-theory structure.

The expression (1.9) for the average cost can be put into a useful alternative form, involving the probability (or probability density) for the decisions $\boldsymbol{\gamma}$ that the system in question makes, thus exhibiting the role of the error probabilities associated with the possible decisions. We let $p(\boldsymbol{\gamma}|\mathbf{S})$ be the probability (or p.d., for extraction) that the system makes a decision $\boldsymbol{\gamma}$ when the signal is $\mathbf{S}$ and a decision rule $\delta(\boldsymbol{\gamma}|\mathbf{V})$ is adopted, so that

$$p(\boldsymbol{\gamma}|\mathbf{S}) = \int_\Gamma F_n(\mathbf{V}|\mathbf{S})\,\delta(\boldsymbol{\gamma}|\mathbf{V})\,\mathbf{dV} \tag{1.13}$$

† Unless otherwise indicated, we adopt the convention that d.d.'s of different arguments are different functions; e.g., $\sigma(\mathbf{S}) \neq \sigma(\boldsymbol{\theta})$.

‡ More explicitly, $\delta(\mathbf{S} - \boldsymbol{\gamma}_\sigma)$ is an n-dimensional delta function: $\delta(S_1 - \gamma_{\sigma 1})\,\delta(S_2 - \gamma_{\sigma 2}) \cdots \delta(S_n - \gamma_{\sigma n})$; Ref. 1, sec. 1.2-4.

Comparison with the *conditional cost or risk* [the expression within the braces { } of Eq. (1.9), which we shall denote by $r(\mathbf{S}, \delta)$] shows that the latter may be written

$$r(\mathbf{S},\delta) = \int_\Delta p(\gamma|\mathbf{S})C(\mathbf{S},\gamma)\, \mathbf{d}\gamma \tag{1.14}$$

which is simply the sum of the costs associated with all possible decisions for the given $\mathbf{S}$, weighted according to their probability of occurrence. The probability (or p.d.) of the decisions γ is therefore

$$p(\gamma) = \langle p(\gamma|\mathbf{S})\rangle_S = \int_\Omega \sigma(\mathbf{S})\, \mathbf{dS} \int_\Gamma F_n(\mathbf{V}|\mathbf{S})\, \delta(\gamma|\mathbf{V})\, \mathbf{dV} \tag{1.15}$$

which is not the same thing, clearly, as the conditional risk (1.14).

Since we are concerned here exclusively with *nonrandomized decision rules* (i.e., specific rules which are not selected on a chance basis but are always the same for all inputs), we may write $\delta(\gamma|\mathbf{V})$ as

$$\delta(\gamma|\mathbf{V}) = \delta(\gamma - \gamma_\sigma(\mathbf{V})) \tag{1.16}$$

with the right-hand member a delta function; cf. Eq. (1.11). Here, however, $\gamma_\sigma(\mathbf{V})$ is in general the functional operation, depending on $\sigma(\mathbf{S})$, which is performed on the data by the system. For extraction, γ_σ is an estimator, as we noted above, while for detection γ_σ may be chosen as some appropriate function of signal and noise statistics, as we shall see in the next chapter when we consider optimum detection. Using Eq. (1.16) in (1.15) and the integral form of the delta function† we have

$$p(\gamma) = \int_{-\infty}^{\infty} \cdots \int \frac{\mathbf{d}\xi}{(2\pi)^m} \int_\Gamma \langle F_n(\mathbf{V}|\mathbf{S})\rangle_S e^{i\tilde{\xi}\gamma - i\tilde{\xi}\gamma_\sigma(\mathbf{V})}\, \mathbf{dV} \tag{1.17}$$

for the probability (or p.d.) of decisions γ, which may represent correct or incorrect decisions. Here the $\langle\ \rangle_S$ on F_n denote the statistical average with respect to $\sigma(\mathbf{S})$, over $\mathbf{S}$, and $\tilde{\xi}$ is a transposed column vector, i.e., a row vector. The relation (1.17) is particularly useful in specific calculations, as we shall see in later chapters.

With Eqs. (1.9) and (1.10) for both detection and extraction we have now obtained a measure of performance for the single-link communication systems embodied in Eq. (1.1). Our next task is to determine optimum systems from extrema of $\mathfrak{L}_1$ and $\mathfrak{L}_2$ by suitable choice of the decision rules.

† Ref. 1, eq. (1.16*b*).

1.3 *Optimization, Extrema, and System Comparisons*[1,8]

Let us now consider in general terms the problem of system optimization. Here, definite decisions are required—either the "yes-no" form typical of the detection situation or as measurements, characteristic of signal extraction. Since the medium of propagation, or channel, $T_M^{(N)}$, is not under our control, we are left with the possible adjustment of receiver ($T_R^{(N)}$), transmitter ($T_T^{(N)}$), or both, in order to achieve optimization. From Eq. (1.1) we may accordingly write

$$\text{op}\,\{v\} = \underset{T_R, T_T}{\text{op}}\,(T_R^{(N)} T_N^{(M)} T_T^{(N)}\{u\}) \tag{1.18}$$

From the viewpoint of the receiver, often the situation in practice, the transmitted processes $y = T_M^{(N)} T_T^{(N)}\{u\}$ are specified (in structure and statistics), so that the only possibilities of optimizing performance depend on suitable choices of $T_R^{(N)}$. Clearly, this is a nontrivial problem because of the inevitable and unavoidable "background noise" that accompanies the desired or possible signals, thus guaranteeing that $T_R^{(N)} \neq T_T^{(N)-1}$. The problem of optimum reception in the light of decision-theoretic methods is also a natural point of application for extremal techniques, especially in cases where the decision itself has primary significance.† However, if the interests of the communication process are more naturally served by maximum use of channel capacity rather than by the significance of the messages sent and received, i.e., than by their outcomes, the principal concern in optimization is then with the encoding process $T_T^{(N)}$, as illustrated by the usual applications of information theory.[6] When both interests can be naturally combined,‡ we may seek some kind of simultaneous adjustment of $T_R^{(N)}$ and $T_T^{(N)}$. Even when specific encoding procedures (over a succession of many individual decisions at the receiver concerning the transmitted symbols) are not themselves directly incorporated into particular $T_T^{(N)}$'s, we may still seek simultaneous adjustments of $T_R^{(N)}$ and $T_T^{(N)}$ for possible further enhancement of performance, a procedure we have earlier called cost coding§ (cf. Sec. 1.1).

Optimization here requires (1) a choice of criterion and (2) selection of the appropriate decision rule. Among the most important and

† Ref. 1, pp. 1065 and 1066.
‡ Ref. 1, sec. 6.5-5.
§ Ref. 1, sec. 23.2.

widely used procedures is the *minimization of average risk or cost*,

$$\mathfrak{L}_1 = R(\sigma,\delta)$$

[Eq. (1.9)]. This is expressed as

$$\min_{\delta} R(\sigma,\delta) = R^*(\sigma,\delta^*) \qquad \delta \rightarrow \delta^* \tag{1.19}$$

and R^* is called the *Bayes risk*, while δ^* is the *Bayes decision rule*, for which R is minimized. Accordingly, here

$$\text{op}\,\{v\} = \underset{\boldsymbol{T}_R}{\text{op}}\,(\boldsymbol{T}_R^{(N)}\boldsymbol{T}_M^{(N)}\boldsymbol{T}_T^{(N)}\{u\} \tag{1.20}$$

yields R^* through the proper choice of $\boldsymbol{T}_{R\text{-op}} \equiv \delta^*$.

A second minimization principle is obtained if $\mathfrak{L}_2 = H$ [Eq. (1.10)] is used in place of $\mathfrak{L}_1$ above. We can write similarly

$$\min_{\delta} H(\sigma,\delta) = H^*(\sigma,\delta_H^*) \qquad \delta \rightarrow \delta_H^* \;(\neq \delta^*, \text{ in general}) \tag{1.21}$$

Equation (1.20) is still representative, with $\boldsymbol{T}_{R\text{-op}}^{(N)} \equiv \delta_H^*$ here; H^* is called the *Bayes equivocation*, or minimum average information loss, and it exists under more restricted conditions than R^*.

A third class of extremum systems of considerable importance is provided by the so-called *Minimax systems*. For cost functions of type 1, i.e., $\mathfrak{F}_1 = C(\mathbf{S},\gamma)$ [Eq. (1.7)], these systems are defined as the least unfavorable of those yielding the worst average costs, the latter being obtained for the most "unfavorable" a priori d.d. σ_0 of the signal process $\mathbf{S}$, namely,

$$R_M^*(\sigma_0,\delta_M^*) = \min_{\delta}\max_{\sigma} R(\sigma,\delta) \tag{1.22}$$

Here, δ_M^* ($\equiv \boldsymbol{T}_{R\text{-op}}^{(N)}$) is the Minimax decision rule $\delta \rightarrow \delta_M^*$. Minimax systems are, of course, more complicated than the simpler Bayes systems (δ^*) that minimize average risk or cost, since a double extremizing process is now required. They also tend to be too conservative on occasion, so that other criteria may be more natural choices.† Subject to conditions readily met in practice,† it is moreover true that

$$\min_{\delta}\max_{\sigma} R(\sigma,\delta) = \max_{\sigma}\min_{\delta} R(\sigma,\delta) \tag{1.23}$$

which in the language of game theory means that we have a *strictly*

† Ref. 1, sec. 18.4-4.

determined, zero-sum, two-person game. Here the game is between the observer (i.e., the receiver) and nature, with a characteristic saddle-point condition represented by Eq. (1.23).†

In a similar way, but under more restrictive conditions, we can expect a *Minimax equivocation*, that is,

$$H_M^*(\sigma_{0H},\delta_{MH}^*) \equiv \min_{\delta} \max_{\sigma} H(\sigma,\delta) = \max_{\sigma} \min_{\delta} H(\sigma,\delta) \qquad (1.24)$$

the last in the strictly determined cases. Hence we have $\delta \to \delta_{MH}^*$ ($\neq \delta_M^*$, generally), and also in general σ_{0H} is different from σ_0.

The criteria of optimality represented by the Bayes and Minimax average risks [Eqs. (1.19), (1.22), and (1.23)] were first proposed and examined by Wald[7] in his original construction of decision theory, along with the principal theorems upon which are based the formal operations presented above.‡

Besides the criteria above, based on $\mathfrak{F}_1$ and $\mathfrak{F}_2$ and without further constraints other than those necessarily imposed through the probabilistic character of decision rules and the a priori probabilities σ, $F_n(\mathbf{V}|\mathbf{S})$, etc., we may briefly mention the extremal situation of cost coding, noting that now additional constraints will naturally arise. Here we seek a possible further minimization of the average risk $R(\sigma,\delta)$ by suitable choice of waveform S, subject, say, to the constraint of fixed average signal power. This can be expressed as

$$R_c^* \equiv \operatorname*{ext}_{S} \, [R^*(\sigma,\delta^*) \not{c} f(S)] = R_c^*(\sigma,\delta_c^*) \qquad (1.25)$$

where $\not{c}$ denotes the constraint. For fixed average signal power this is

$$f(S) = \frac{1}{T}\int_0^T \langle S(t)\rangle^2 \, dt \qquad (1.26)$$

We thus adjust $\boldsymbol{T}_T^{(N)}$ and $\boldsymbol{T}_R^{(N)}$ to achieve R_c^*, the former by choice of waveform at the transmitter, the latter, by minimizing the average risk for this waveform, at the receiver. In general, this minimization of an already Bayes risk is not unique, nor is it always possible.[8]

System comparisons are now readily effected in principle: the most common is to compare the average and Bayes risks for a suboptimum system δ and an optimal one δ^*, respectively, viz.,

$$R^*(\sigma,\delta^*) \quad \text{vs.} \quad R(\sigma,\delta) \qquad R^* < R \qquad (1.27)$$

† Ref. 1, sec. 23.3.
‡ Ref. 1, sec. 18.5.

In detail, this is usually expressed in terms of the pertinent system parameters by determining how much weaker an input signal is required, or how much shorter an observation time is needed, to yield the same average cost or risk in the two cases. Similarly, one can compare system performance on the basis of the appropriate probabilities themselves of decision $p(\gamma)$ [cf. Eq. (1.15)] for δ and δ^*, where now γ, γ^* [cf. Eq. (1.16)] are respectively the suboptimum and optimum systems in question. Similar remarks apply for the other criteria: Bayes equivocation, Minimax, etc. Although in the subsequent chapters we shall confine our attention to minimum average risk (i.e., Bayes) systems, it is evident that the same philosophy applies to optimum and suboptimum systems with respect to the other criteria cited above.

1.4 Remarks

In the preceding sections we have outlined a general theory for the basic single-link communication system of Eq. (1.1), using decision-theory methods. Our principal aims have been to incorporate the fundamental objectives of optimum system design, evaluation, and comparison of performance into a single, quantitative model. This is formally achieved for signal detection and signal extraction once optimum decision rules δ^*, δ_M^*, etc., are found, with system evaluation measured in the corresponding Bayes risks, or Minimax risks, etc. The optimum decision rule (δ^*, etc.) embodies the structure of the optimum system. It is one principal aim of our subsequent discussion to obtain such structures explicitly (Chaps. 2 and 3 for detection and extraction, respectively), and to show how the structures, as a set of definite analytical operations on the received data (V), can be interpreted as ordered series of realizable physical elements (Chap. 4). In addition to the question of optimum structure, a second important goal of our study is to obtain the decision probabilities $p(\gamma)$, including probabilities of error, and the Bayes risks (minimum average costs) associated with these optimum systems. We note the critical role played by a priori information, here represented by the statistical properties of signal and noise through $\sigma(\mathbf{S})$ and $F_n(\mathbf{V}|\mathbf{S})$ [see Eqs. (1.2)]. These and the manner in which signal and noise are combined ($S \otimes N$) embody the "physics" of the class of communication problems under consideration. We accordingly expect that changes in these a priori data will modify the optimum structure as well as the expected performance. Just how much is another, more general aim of the present theory, which we will discuss in a somewhat more detailed manner in Chap. 5.

We emphasize that our present model is by no means the most general, although the Bayes theory (minimum average risk, etc.) is probably the simplest that combines in a natural and appropriate way the various notions of optimality, evaluation, and structure that are the minimum desiderata of an adequate theory. More complicated criteria can be selected (for example, some of those appearing in the cost-coding cases [cf. Eqs. (1.25) and (1.26)] and in the more involved min-max–min-min problems, etc.[8]), but their greater "realism" is usually dearly bought at the price of analytical difficulty. We also remark that the Bayes theory formally presented in the outline above has its original mathematical foundation primarily in the work of Wald.[7] The necessary theorems are summarized in Ref. 1, chap. 18, where these and related topics are considered in much greater detail. We turn now, therefore, to the explicit problems of optimum signal detection, discussed in Chap. 2, and optimum signal extraction, treated in Chap. 3, where we shall attempt to cover the bones of abstract formulation with the muscle of specific results.

References

1. Middleton, D.: "An Introduction to Statistical Communication Theory," McGraw-Hill Book Company, New York, 1960.
2. Bartlett, M. S.: "An Introduction to Stochastic Processes," Cambridge University Press, London, 1955.
3. Middleton, D., and D. Van Meter: Detection and Extraction of Signals in Noise from the Point of View of Statistical Decision Theory, *J. Soc. Ind. Appl. Math.*, **3**(4):192 (1955) and **4**(2):86 (1956).
4. Wiener, N.: "Extrapolation, Interpolation, and Smoothing of Stationary Time Series," The Technology Press of the Massachusetts Institute of Technology, Cambridge, Mass., and John Wiley & Sons, Inc., New York, 1949.
5. Kolmogoroff, A. N.: Interpolation and Extrapolation, *Bull. Acad. Sci. USSR, Math. Ser.*, **5**:3–14 (1944).
6. Shannon, C. E.: A Mathematical Theory of Communication, *Bell System Tech. J.*, **27**:379, 623 (1948).
7. Wald, A.: "Statistical Decision Functions," John Wiley & Sons, Inc., New York, 1950.
8. Middleton, D.: Optimization Problems in Statistical Communication Theory, in R. Bellman (ed.): "Mathematical Optimization Techniques," chap. 7, University of California Press, Berkeley, Calif., 1963.

Chapter 2

The Detection of Signals in Noise

The first important topic in communication theory to which we shall apply the decision-theory methods described in Chap. 1 is the detection of signals in noise.† Here we are concerned mainly with optimum detection in the sense of minimum average cost or risk (cf. Sec. 1.3). Accordingly, we wish to determine $T_R^{(N)} = (T_R^{(N)})_{\text{det}}$ for these optimum systems and to obtain the associated error probabilities and Bayes risks. Our discussion below includes system comparisons (e.g., optimum versus suboptimum), various types of optimality, a number of canonical results, and several simple examples, to illustrate the formal structure of the detection theory whose development is the principal aim of this chapter.[1,5,9,10,11]

2.1 *Formulation: Error Probabilities and Average Risks*

Let us begin by considering the *binary* (i.e., two-alternative) situation of distinguishing between the presence of a signal of type S in noise N

† For a brief account of the development of this subject from the modern statistical viewpoint, see the footnote on p. 801 of Ref. 1.

vis-à-vis noise N alone, which may occur alternatively. This is a test of the statistical hypothesis H_1: $S \otimes N$ versus the hypothesis H_0: N. Before we can obtain the optimum system and its Bayes risk, we must first construct the average risk for this test on the basis of a fixed number of data samples in $(0,T)$. For this purpose we have

$$\Omega_0 + \Omega_1 = \Omega \tag{2.1a}$$

where Ω_0 and Ω_1 are respectively the signal spaces for the null signal $(S_0 = 0)$ and for signals of class S_1 $(\neq 0)$. We assume for the present that these signal spaces are disjoint, i.e., are nonoverlapping: no points of Ω_1 fall in Ω_0, and vice versa; Ω_0, Ω_1 are also called *hypothesis classes*,† and our binary test of H_1: $S \otimes N$ versus H_0: N is equivalently H_1: $S_1 \epsilon \Omega_1$ versus H_0: $S_0 \epsilon \Omega_0$. The class Ω_1 may contain one or more distinguishable members—in fact, infinitely many—while Ω_0 contains only one, the null signal.

Next we have

$$w_1(\mathbf{S}_1),\ w_0(\mathbf{S}) = \text{d.d's of } \mathbf{S} = \mathbf{S}_1 \qquad \text{and} \qquad \mathbf{S}_0 = 0$$

with

$$\int_{\Omega_1} w_1(\mathbf{S})\, d\mathbf{S} = 1 \qquad \int_{\Omega_0} w_0(\mathbf{S})\, d\mathbf{S} = 1 \qquad w_0(\mathbf{S}) = \delta(\mathbf{S} - \mathbf{0}) \tag{2.1b}$$

p, q = a priori probabilities that the data sample $\mathbf{V}$ comes from the ensemble

$$V = S_1 \otimes N \qquad \text{or} \qquad V = N \qquad \text{respectively}$$
$$\text{with} \qquad p + q = 1 \tag{2.1c}$$

Consequently, we can write for the a priori d.d. of all signals in signal space Ω

$$\sigma(\mathbf{S}) = q\,\delta(\mathbf{S} - \mathbf{0}) + p w_1(\mathbf{S})$$
$$\text{and} \qquad \int_\Omega \sigma(\mathbf{S})\, \mathbf{dS} = 1 \tag{2.2}$$

by virtue of Eqs. (2.1*b*) and (2.1*c*). For the two possible decisions here, namely, γ_1: H_1 and γ_0: H_0, we must have the following relation for the decision rules δ:

$$\delta(\gamma_0|\mathbf{V}) + \delta(\gamma_1|\mathbf{V}) = 1 \tag{2.3}$$

† Ref. 1, sec. 18.2-1.

since a definite decision is always made and $0 \leq \delta_1, \delta_2 \leq 1$, inasmuch as the δ's are probabilities in the detection situation (Sec. 1.2).

At this point we choose $\mathfrak{F}_1 = C(\mathbf{S},\gamma)$ as our cost function [cf. Eq. (1.7)]. For the binary cases considered here there are four cost assignments: two for the possible correct decisions and two for the possible incorrect decisions. It is convenient to represent them by a *cost matrix* $\mathbf{C}(\mathbf{S},\gamma)$:

$$\mathbf{C}(\mathbf{S},\gamma) = \begin{bmatrix} C_0^{(0)} & C_1^{(0)} \\ C_0^{(1)} & C_1^{(1)} \end{bmatrix} \tag{2.4}$$

where the rows represent the hypotheses H_0, H_1 and the columns the decisions γ_0, γ_1. The superscripts refer to the hypothesis state and the subscripts to the decision actually made. Consistent with the meanings of "correct" (i.e., "success") and "incorrect" ("failure"), with respect to the possible decisions, we require that

$$C_0^{(0)} < C_1^{(0)} \qquad C_1^{(1)} < C_0^{(1)} \tag{2.5}$$

i.e., "failure" costs more than "success." Observe that the costs are assigned vis-à-vis the possible hypothesis states (or signal classes) and not with respect to any one signal in a signal class (which in the case of composite hypotheses contains more than one member).

The average cost or risk may now be found from Eq. (1.9) by integrating over the two points (γ_1,γ_2) in the decision space Δ. The result is

$$\begin{aligned} R(\sigma,\delta) = \int_\Gamma \{ [qC_0^{(0)}F_n(\mathbf{V}|\mathbf{0}) + pC_0^{(1)}\langle F_n(\mathbf{V}|\mathbf{S}_1)\rangle_1] \, \delta(\gamma_0|\mathbf{V}) \\ + [qC_1^{(0)}F_n(\mathbf{V}|\mathbf{0}) + pC_1^{(1)}\langle F_n(\mathbf{V}|\mathbf{S}_1)\rangle_1] \, \delta(\gamma_1|\mathbf{V}) \} \, \mathbf{dV} \end{aligned} \tag{2.6}$$

where

$$\begin{aligned} p\langle F_n(\mathbf{V}|\mathbf{S}_1)\rangle_1 &= \int_{\Omega_1} \sigma(\mathbf{S}) F_n(\mathbf{V}|\mathbf{S}) \, \mathbf{dS} \\ &= p \int_{S_1} w_1(\mathbf{S}_1) F_n(\mathbf{V}|\mathbf{S}_1) \, \mathbf{dS}_1 \end{aligned} \tag{2.7}$$

When the signal processes owe their statistical character alone to a set of random parameters $\boldsymbol{\theta}$, that is, when the signals are deterministic (a usual case in practice), then Eq. (2.7) takes the equivalent form

$$p\langle F_n(\mathbf{V}|\mathbf{S}_1)\rangle_1 = p \int_{\theta_1} w(\boldsymbol{\theta}_1) F_n(\mathbf{V}|\mathbf{S}_1(\boldsymbol{\theta}_1)) \, \mathbf{d}\boldsymbol{\theta}_1 \tag{2.7a}$$

The average cost Eq. (2.6) can be more compactly expressed in terms of the error probabilities and probabilities of correct decision. We start by introducing the conditional and total error probabilities:

$$\beta_1^{(0)} \equiv \beta_1^{(0)}(\gamma_1|H_0) = \text{conditional probability of incorrectly deciding that a signal is present when only noise occurs (type 1 error probability)} \tag{2.8a}$$

$$\beta_0^{(1)} \equiv \beta_0^{(1)}(\gamma_0|H_1) = \text{conditional probability of incorrectly deciding that only noise occurs when a signal is also present (type 2 error probability)} \tag{2.8b}$$

The corresponding total error probabilities are accordingly $q\beta_1^{(0)}$, $p\beta_0^{(1)}$. In expanded form we have

$$\begin{aligned} \beta_1^{(0)} &= \int_\Gamma F_n(\mathbf{V}|\mathbf{0})\, \delta(\gamma_1|\mathbf{V})\, d\mathbf{V} \\ \beta_0^{(1)} &= \int_\Gamma \langle F_n(\mathbf{V}|\mathbf{S}_1)\rangle_1\, \delta(\gamma_0|\mathbf{V})\, d\mathbf{V} \end{aligned} \tag{2.9}$$

so that, alternatively, the conditional probabilities of correct decisions are

$$\beta_0^{(0)} \equiv \beta_0^{(0)}(\gamma_0|H_0) = 1 - \beta_1^{(0)} = \int_\Gamma F_n(\mathbf{V}|\mathbf{0})\, \delta(\gamma_0|\mathbf{V})\, d\mathbf{V} \tag{2.10a}$$

$$\beta_1^{(1)} \equiv \beta_1^{(1)}(\gamma_1|H_1) = 1 - \beta_0^{(1)} = \int_\Gamma \langle F_n(\mathbf{V}|\mathbf{S}_1)\rangle_1\, \delta(\gamma_1|\mathbf{V})\, d\mathbf{V} \tag{2.10b}$$

where we have used Eq. (2.3). Applying Eqs. (2.2) to Eq. (1.15) for the total probability of a decision $\gamma = \gamma_0$: H_0, no signal, or $\gamma = \gamma_1 = H_1$, a signal in noise, we find, respectively, that

$$\begin{aligned} p(\gamma_0) &= \int_\Gamma [qF_n(\mathbf{V}|\mathbf{0}) + p\langle F_n(\mathbf{V}|\mathbf{S}_1)\rangle_1]\, \delta(\gamma_0|\mathbf{V})\, d\mathbf{V} \\ &= q\beta_0^{(0)} + p\beta_0^{(1)} \end{aligned} \tag{2.11a}$$

and similarly

$$p(\gamma_1) = q\beta_1^{(0)} + p\beta_1^{(1)} \tag{2.11b}$$

as expected. [Note that $p(\gamma_0) + p(\gamma_1) = 1$.]

With the help of Eqs. (2.8) to (2.11) in Eq. (2.6) we can now represent the average risk $R(\sigma,\delta)$ more compactly as

$$R(\sigma,\delta) = \{qC_0^{(0)} + pC_1^{(1)}\} + q(C_1^{(0)} - C_0^{(0)})\, \beta_1^{(0)} + p(C_0^{(1)} - C_1^{(1)})\beta_0^{(1)} \tag{2.12}$$

in terms of the type 1 and 2 *error* probabilities, or as

$$R(\sigma,\delta) = \{qC_1^{(0)} + pC_0^{(1)}\} - q(C_1^{(0)} - C_0^{(0)})\beta_0^{(0)} - p(C_0^{(1)} - C_1^{(1)})\beta_1^{(1)} \tag{2.13}$$

in terms of the probabilities of *correct* decisions.

2.2 $S_1 \oplus N$ *versus* $S_2 \oplus N$: *Overlapping Hypothesis Classes*

It is instructive now to extend the "on-off" binary case of Sec. 2.1 to the more general situation of detecting the presence of a signal of class S_2 in noise vis-à-vis that of a signal of class S_1, also in noise. The statistical hypotheses are H_2: $S_2 \oplus N$ versus H_1: $S_1 \oplus N$. Unlike the "on-off" case of Sec. 2.1, where the hypotheses classes were required always to be disjoint, we distinguish two different cases here: (1) nonoverlapping signal classes and (2) overlapping, or nondisjoint, signal classes. For the former the generalization of the preceding formulation is quite straightforward, as noted below. For the latter, however, a somewhat more sophisticated viewpoint is required.

We consider first the simpler case of disjoint signal classes. There Eq. (2.1*a*) applies, with Ω_0 replaced by Ω_2 and the appropriate description. In place of Eqs. (2.2), however, we have

$$\sigma(\mathbf{S}) = p_1 w_1(\mathbf{S}_1) + p_2 w_2(\mathbf{S}_2) \qquad \text{and} \qquad \int_\Omega \sigma(\mathbf{S})\, d\mathbf{S} = 1 \tag{2.14}$$

with $p_1 + p_2 = 1$, and p_1, p_2 the respective a priori probabilities of a signal of class 1 (or 2) occurring in the data sample $\mathbf{V}$. Here

$$\int_{\Omega_1} w_1(\mathbf{S}_1)\, d\mathbf{S} = \int_{\Omega_2} w_2(\mathbf{S}_2)\, d\mathbf{S} = 1 \tag{2.15}$$

with w_1, w_2 the d.d.'s of $\mathbf{S}_1$ and $\mathbf{S}_2$ (or their respective statistical parameters). Equation (2.3) is modified in an obvious way, as is the cost matrix (2.4) and the condition (2.5), which becomes

$$C_1^{(1)} < C_2^{(1)} \qquad C_2^{(2)} < C_1^{(2)}$$

to ensure the required greater cost of "failure" vis-à-vis "success." The average risk (2.6) is now modified to

$$\begin{aligned} R(\sigma,\delta) = \int \{ & [p_1 C_1^{(1)} \langle F_n(\mathbf{V}|\mathbf{S}_1)\rangle_1 + p_2 C_1^{(2)} \langle F_n(\mathbf{V}|\mathbf{S}_2)\rangle_2]\, \delta(\gamma_1|\mathbf{V}) \\ & + [p_1 C_2^{(1)} \langle F_n(\mathbf{V}|\mathbf{S}_1)\rangle_1 + p_2 C_2^{(2)} \langle F_n(\mathbf{V}|\mathbf{S}_2)\rangle_2]\, \delta(\gamma_2|\mathbf{V})\}\, d\mathbf{V} \end{aligned} \tag{2.16}$$

where now

$$p_1\langle F_n(\mathbf{V}|\mathbf{S}_1)\rangle_1 = \int_{\Omega_1} \sigma(\mathbf{S})F_n(\mathbf{V}|\mathbf{S}_1)\,d\mathbf{S} = p_1 \int_{S_1} w_1(\mathbf{S}_1)F_n(\mathbf{V}|\mathbf{S}_1)\,d\mathbf{S}_1 \tag{2.17}$$

etc., with Eq. (2.7*a*) suitably altered for the case where the signals are deterministic, with random parameters $\boldsymbol{\theta}_1$, $\boldsymbol{\theta}_2$.

The error probabilities are similarly modified:

$$\beta_2^{(1)} \equiv \beta_2^{(1)}(\gamma_2|H_1) = \text{conditional probability of incorrectly deciding that a signal of class 2 is present when actually a signal of type 1 occurs} \tag{2.18}$$

etc., for $\beta_1^{(2)}$, the total error probabilities, and total probabilities of deciding γ_1 or γ_2. The average risk (2.16) takes the compact form

$$R(\sigma,\delta) = \{p_1C_1^{(1)} + p_2C_2^{(2)}\} + p_1(C_2^{(1)} - C_1^{(1)})\beta_2^{(1)} + p_2(C_1^{(2)} - C_2^{(2)})\beta_1^{(2)} \tag{2.19}$$

with an expression equivalent to (2.13), in terms of the probabilities of correct decisions.

When the signal classes are not disjoint, the usual definitions of correct and incorrect decisions are no longer valid, since it is no longer certain whether or not an error has been made. Let us suppose, for example, that signal class S_1 consists of deterministic signals of the type $S(\boldsymbol{\theta}_1)$ and signal class S_2 of the type $S(\boldsymbol{\theta}_2)$, where the *waveforms* (S) of the two classes are the same and each has the same type of random parameter(s); e.g., $\boldsymbol{\theta}_1$, $\boldsymbol{\theta}_2 = \boldsymbol{\theta}$ in both instances represent the same set of random parameters, but with different distribution densities, $w_1(\boldsymbol{\theta}) \neq w_2(\boldsymbol{\theta})$. Any given signal S may belong to either signal class, but S will usually belong to one class with greater probability than to the other. It is reasonable to assign to the more probable decision a lesser cost. Thus, if $\boldsymbol{\theta} = a$ represents a random amplitude, for instance, and if the amplitude a of a particular S lies close to the mean value of $w_1(a)$ but well out on the "tail" of $w_2(a)$, a larger value is assigned to the loss function $\mathfrak{F}(S,\gamma_2)$ than to the loss function $\mathfrak{F}(S,\gamma_1)$ for the more probably correct decision.

Accordingly, it is clear that the cost assignment should be related to the probability that the signal belongs to *each* of the signal classes. This can be accomplished in a variety of ways, but the simplest is to require specifically that (1) $\mathfrak{F}(S,\gamma)$ be continuous in the prior probabilities (p_1,p_2,w_1,w_2) and (2) that $\mathfrak{F}(S,\gamma)$ reduce to the usual cost assignments whenever the signal belongs to a disjoint signal class. For the systems considered here, based on constant, preset costs, an extension of the "constant" cost function $\mathfrak{F}_1$, Eq. (1.7), satisfying these conditions is[2]

$$C(S,\gamma_i) = [C_1^{(i)}p_1w_1(\boldsymbol{\theta}) + C_2^{(i)}p_2w_2(\boldsymbol{\theta})]/\sigma(\boldsymbol{\theta}) \qquad 1 = 1, 2 \quad (2.20)$$

where $\sigma(\boldsymbol{\theta}) = p_1w_1(\boldsymbol{\theta}) + p_2w_2(\boldsymbol{\theta})$ is the prior d.d. of $\boldsymbol{\theta}$ for deterministic signals $S(\boldsymbol{\theta})$. In general we have

$$C(S,\gamma_i) = [C_1^{(i)}p_1w_1(\mathbf{S}) + C_2^{(i)}p_2w_2(\mathbf{S})]/\sigma(\mathbf{S}) \qquad (2.21)$$

with $\sigma(\mathbf{S})$ given by Eqs. (2.14). Thus, by a similar argument Eq. (2.21) applies for the case of completely stochastic signals $\mathbf{S}$, where now $w_1(\mathbf{S}) \neq w_2(\mathbf{S})$. With Eqs. (2.20) and (2.21) the average risk $R(\sigma,\delta)$ reduces to the original expression (2.16) for disjoint classes.† In this way we unite the treatment of overlapping and nonoverlapping signal classes, employing the formalism of the latter as before but now including all the signal types of practical interest.

2.3 *Optimum Detection*

The criterion of optimization here (and subsequently) is chosen to be the minimization of average risk [cf. Eq. (1.19)]. Thus, by suitable choice of decision rule δ_0 [or δ_1, since δ_0 and δ_1 are related by Eq. (2.3) in these binary cases], the average risk $R(\sigma,\delta)$, Eq. (2.6) or (2.12), is minimized by making the error probabilities as small as possible, consistent with Eq. (2.3) and the constraint (2.5) on the preassigned costs.‡ We assume here, also, that the cost function $C(\mathbf{S},\gamma)$ is chosen according to Eq. (2.21) [or (2.20)], so that overlapping hypothesis (or signal) classes are included. This allows us to treat stochastic signals, as well as all classes of deterministic signals, in the present theory.

Eliminating $\delta(\gamma_1|\mathbf{V})$ with the help of Eq. (2.3), we may express Eq. (2.6) as

$$R(\sigma,\delta) = \mathcal{R}_0 + p(C_0^{(1)} - C_1^{(1)}) \int_\Gamma \delta(\gamma_0|\mathbf{V})[\Lambda_n(\mathbf{V}) - \mathcal{K}_{01}]F_n(\mathbf{V}|\mathbf{0})\, d\mathbf{V} \qquad (2.22)$$

† Overlapping classes involving the null signal $S = 0$ (noise alone) are similarly handled, with $C(S,\gamma_i) = [C_0^{(i)}qw_0(\mathbf{S}) + C_1^{(i)}pw_1(\mathbf{S})]/\sigma(\mathbf{S})$, $i = 0, 1$, and with $\sigma(\mathbf{S})$ given by Eqs. (2.2) and $R(\sigma,\delta)$ by Eq. (2.6), etc.

‡ Equivalently, $R(\sigma,\delta)$ is minimized by *maximizing* the probabilities of correct decisions; cf. Eq. (2.13).

where

$$\Lambda_n(\mathbf{V}) \equiv \frac{p}{q} \frac{\langle F_n(\mathbf{V}|\mathbf{S}_1)\rangle_1}{F_n(\mathbf{V}|\mathbf{0})} \tag{2.23}$$

is a *generalized likelihood ratio* and $\mathcal{K}_{01}$ is a *threshold:*

$$\mathcal{K}_{01} \equiv \frac{C_1^{(0)} - C_0^{(0)}}{C_0^{(1)} - C_1^{(1)}} (>0) \tag{2.24}$$

with $\mathcal{R}_0 = qC_0^{(0)} + pC_1^{(1)}$ the *irreducible risk*. Since δ_0, $F_n(\mathbf{V}|0)$, $C_0^{(1)} - C_1^{(1)}$, p, etc., are all positive (or zero), we see directly that R can be minimized by choosing $\delta(\gamma_0|\mathbf{V}) \to \delta^*(\gamma_0|\mathbf{V})$ to be unity when $\Lambda_n < \mathcal{K}_{01}$ and zero when $\Lambda_n > \mathcal{K}_{01}$. Thus, we decide

γ_0: H_0 if $\Lambda_n(\mathbf{V}) < \mathcal{K}_{01}$

namely, we set $\delta^*(\gamma_0|\mathbf{V}) = 1$ for any $\mathbf{V}$ that yields this inequality. From Eq. (2.3) this means also that

$$\delta^*(\gamma_1|\mathbf{V}) = 0 \tag{2.25a}$$

The region of Γ for which $\delta_0^* = 1$, $\delta_1^* = 0$ is Γ_0; i.e., Γ_0 contains all $\mathbf{V}$ satisfying the inequality $\Lambda_n(\mathbf{V}) < \mathcal{K}_{01}$.

Or we decide

γ_1: H_1 if $\Lambda_n(\mathbf{V}) \geq \mathcal{K}_{01}$

that is, we choose $\delta^*(\gamma_1|\mathbf{V}) = 1$ for all $\mathbf{V}$ satisfying this inequality (and equality) and consequently require that

$$\delta^*(\gamma_0|\mathbf{V}) = 0 \tag{2.25b}$$

Here Γ_1 denotes the region of Γ for which

$$\delta_0^* = 0 \qquad \delta_1^* = 1$$

We remark that $\delta_{1,0}^*$ are nonrandomized decision rules, directly deduced from the minimization process itself. From Eqs. (2.9) for these optimum rules we may write the Bayes, or minimum average, risk as

$$R^*(\sigma,\delta^*) = \mathcal{R}_0 + p(C_0^{(1)} - C_1^{(1)}) \left[\frac{\mathcal{K}_{01}}{\mu} \beta_1^{(0)*} + \beta_0^{(1)*} \right] \qquad \mu \equiv p/q \tag{2.26}$$

In actual applications it is usually much more convenient to replace the likelihood ratio Λ_n by its logarithm, as we shall see presently.

This in no way changes the optimum character of the test, since any monotonic function of Λ_n (≥ 0) may serve as test function. Thus, the optimum decision process [Eqs. (2.25*a*) and (2.25*b*)] is simply reexpressed as

Decide
γ_0: H_0 if $\log \Lambda_n < \log \mathcal{K}_{01}$, with

$$\delta^*(\gamma_0|\mathbf{V}) = 1 \qquad \delta^*(\gamma_1|\mathbf{V}) = 0$$

or (2.27)
Decide
γ_1: H_1 if $\log \Lambda_n \geq \log \mathcal{K}_{01}$, with

$$\delta^*(\gamma_0|\mathbf{V}) = 0 \qquad \delta^*(\gamma_1|\mathbf{V}) = 1$$

The likelihood ratio and, equivalently here, its logarithm embody the actual receiver structure $T_R^{(N)}$; viz., the operation the detector must

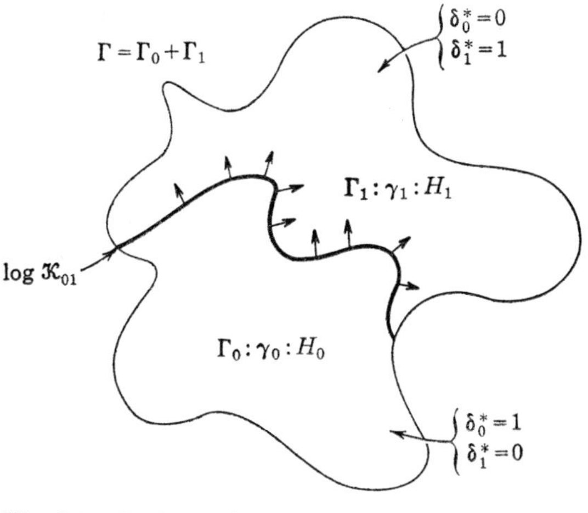

Fig. 2.1 Optimum detection.

perform on the received data $\mathbf{V}$ in order to reach an optimal decision as to the presence or absence of a signal (of class S_1) in noise. The optimum detection situation is schematically illustrated in Fig. 2.1.

While any monotonic function of Λ_n can be used, the logarithm has important special properties that make it particularly suited to the desired optimum receiver structure. First, in a general way, taking the logarithm of the likelihood ratio essentially replaces exponential operations on $\mathbf{V}$ by sums of simple powers of $\mathbf{V}$ or, more succinctly, replaces powers of products by sums of products, with a consequent simplification in actual structure. Now in most practical cases† explicit closed forms of Λ_n (or $\log \Lambda_n$) cannot be obtained, and suitable approximations must then be developed. It turns out that the function of Λ_n to be approximated, in such a way as still to exhibit Bayes (or optimum) properties, is the logarithm. We shall say more about this in Sec. 2.7. Finally, from the standpoint of information theory‡ $\log \Lambda_n$ is proportional to the measure of the difference between uncertainties about the states H_0 and H_1 when $\mathbf{V}$ is known, viz.,

$$\log \Lambda_n(\mathbf{V}) = [-\log qF_n(\mathbf{V}|\mathbf{0})] - [-\log p\langle F_n(\mathbf{V}|\mathbf{S}_1)\rangle_1] \quad (2.28)$$

Thus we see that the decision rule (2.25*a*) and (2.25*b*), or (2.27), is equivalent to deciding in favor of H_1 when the uncertainty in H_1 is less than the uncertainty about H_0 by an amount $\log \mathcal{K}_{01}$.

Important special cases of the general Bayes detection system described above are distinguished. The so-called *Neyman-Pearson detector*§ is one example, where the average risk associated with one or the other error probabilities $\beta_1^{(0)}$ (or $\beta_0^{(1)}$) is held fixed (usually the type 1 error probability $\beta_1^{(0)}$), thereby determining a threshold $\mathcal{K}'$, while the average risk associated with $\beta_0^{(1)}$ (or $\beta_1^{(0)}$) is minimized. As one example we have

$$R^*(\sigma,\delta^*)_{NP} = C_0\{\min_{\delta} p\beta_0^{(1)} + \lambda\beta_1^{(0)}\} \quad (2.29)$$

The result, $\delta \to \delta_{NP}^*$, is easily shown to be a Bayes, i.e., a likelihood-ratio, test of the type (2.25) or (2.27) where $\lambda = \mathcal{K}'$, a threshold determined by the preset value $\beta_1^{(0)}$. A similar argument applies when $\beta_0^{(1)}$ is held fixed and $\beta_1^{(0)}$ is minimized.

Another optimum class of binary detection systems subsumed under the Bayes theory is that of the *Ideal Observer*,‖ where both $\beta_1^{(0)}$ and

† Ref. 1, sec. 19.4 and chap. 20.
‡ Ref. 1, secs. 6.2 and 19.1-3.
§ Ref. 1, sec. 19.2-1.
‖ Ref. 1, sec. 19.2-2.

$\beta_0^{(1)}$ are *jointly* minimized, e.g.,

$$R^*(\sigma,\delta^*)_I = C_0 \min_{\delta} \{q\beta_1^{(0)} + p\beta_0^{(1)}\} \tag{2.30}$$

Here it is found that the decision process requires a threshold $\mathcal{K}_I = 1$. Other classes of Bayes detectors are *Minimax systems* [cf. Eq. (1.22)], where the a priori probabilities p, q are unknown or unspecified. Once again $T_{R\text{-}opt}^{(N)}$ is embodied in a generalized likelihood ratio (2.23). The actual evaluation of such systems, however, may be quite difficult, particularly if other a priori probabilities or probability densities are open to adjustment—for instance, $\sigma(\mathbf{S})$, $\sigma(\boldsymbol{\theta})$, $F_n(\mathbf{V}|\mathbf{S})$. We remark that the Neyman-Pearson detector is customarily used in those situations where it is natural to set an acceptable level of type 1 error rates and operate so as to minimize the type 2 error probability, as in many radar applications.† On the other hand, for many communication systems (radio, etc.) where errors of both types are equally significant, the Ideal Observer is the more suitable optimum structure.

Other extensions are also possible. One important class is described by sequential detection systems where sample size, n, is allowed to vary while $\beta_1^{(0)}$ and $\beta_0^{(1)}$ are preset. Sample size is now the random variable (as well as $\mathbf{V}$), and optimization is accomplished by minimizing the average "cost of experimentation," proportional to sample size. For example, we have for the Bayes risk here

$$R^*_{\text{seq}} = q\alpha C_1^{(0)} + p\beta C_0^{(1)} + pc_0 \min_{\delta} \overline{n(\mathbf{V}|S,\delta)}^{V} \tag{2.31}$$

where the $\overline{}^{V}$ denotes the average over the received data $\mathbf{V}$, c_0 is the "per unit trial" cost of experimentation, and $\alpha = \beta_1^{(0)}$ and $\beta = \beta_0^{(1)}$. In many cases (but not all), $\delta \rightarrow \delta^*_{\text{seq}}$ yields a likelihood detector for the optimum structure.

If $x_s (= \log \Lambda_{n^*})$ is this likelihood detector, then the test procedure involves a *double* threshold, instead of the single threshold characteristic of the fixed-sample test described above [cf. Eqs. (2.25), (2.27)]. The detection process is

$$\begin{aligned} B = \beta/(1-\alpha) < x_s < A = \frac{1-\beta}{\alpha} \quad & \text{test continues} \\ x_s \geq A \quad & \text{test terminates, deciding } H_1 \\ x_s \leq B \quad & \text{test terminates, deciding } H_0 \end{aligned} \tag{2.31a}$$

† An important example is the CFAR (constant false-alarm rate) detector.

Sequential detectors for communication theory problems were considered originally by Bussgang and Middleton.[3]

2.4 *Error Probabilities and System Comparisons*

Before optimum performance can be evaluated we must determine the error probabilities, explicitly from the decision rules (2.27). This is done by evaluating $\beta_1^{(0)*}$ and $\beta_0^{(1)*}$ in Eq. (2.26) over those portions

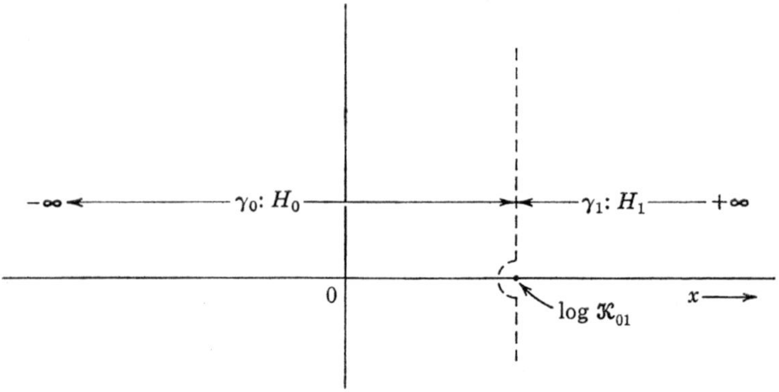

Fig. 2.2 Optimum detection.

of the data space Γ for which $\delta^*(\gamma_0|\mathbf{V}), \delta^*(\gamma_1|\mathbf{V}) = 1$, respectively. Letting

$$x = \log \Lambda_n(\mathbf{V}) = T_{R\text{-opt}}^{(N)}\{\mathbf{V}\} \tag{2.32}$$

we find that these error probabilities are given by

$$\beta_1^{(0)*} = \int_{\log \mathcal{K}_{01}}^{\infty} P_n^{(0)}(x)\, dx \qquad \beta_0^{(1)*} = \int_{-\infty}^{\log \mathcal{K}_{01}} P_n^{(1)}(x)\, dx \tag{2.33}$$

where $P_n^{(0),(1)}$ (x) are the d.d.'s of x, with respect to H_0, H_1. Figure 2.2 shows the optimum detection situation (2.27), based on Eq. (2.32) (cf. Figure 2.1), and Figure 2.3 sketches a typical relationship between $P_n^{(0)}$, etc., and the Bayes error probabilities. The d.d.'s $P_n^{(0),(1)}$ are found from†

$$P_n^{(0)}(x) = \mathfrak{F}^{-1}\{E_{V|H_0}[e^{i\xi x}]\} \tag{2.34a}$$
$$P_n^{(1)}(x) = \mathfrak{F}^{-1}\{E_{V|H_1}[e^{i\xi x}]\} \tag{2.34b}$$

† Ref. 1, sec. 19.3-1.

where $\mathfrak{F}^{-1}$ denotes the inverse Fourier transform and the expectations are the two characteristic functions of x, which are determined explicitly from

$$F_x^{(0)}(i\xi) = \int_\Gamma d\mathbf{V}\, F_n(\mathbf{V}|\mathbf{0})e^{i\xi \log \Lambda_n(\mathbf{V})} \tag{2.35a}$$

and

$$F_x^{(1)}(i\xi) = \int_\Gamma d\mathbf{V}\, \langle F_n(\mathbf{V}|\mathbf{S}_1)\rangle_1 e^{i\xi \log \Lambda_n(\mathbf{V})} \tag{2.35b}$$

In terms of these characteristic functions, $F_x^{(0),(1)}$, the error probabilities can also be expressed equivalently as

$$\begin{aligned} \beta_1^{(0)*} &= \int_{C^{(-)}} \frac{e^{-i\xi \log \mathcal{K}_{01}}}{2\pi i\xi} F_x^{(0)}(i\xi)\, d\xi \\ \beta_0^{(1)*} &= \int_{C^{(+)}} \frac{e^{-i\xi \log \mathcal{K}_{01}}}{-2\pi i\xi} F_x^{(1)}(i\xi)\, d\xi \end{aligned} \tag{2.36}$$

where $C^{(-)}$ and $C^{(+)}$, respectively, are contours extending from $-\infty$ to $+\infty$ along the real axis and indented downward and upward about

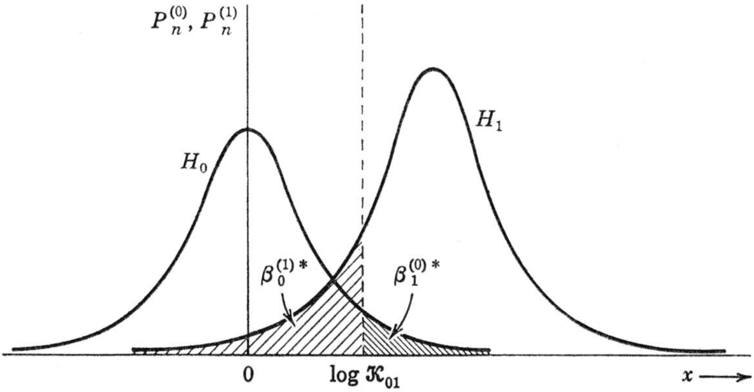

Fig. 2.3 The Bayes error probabilities.

any singularities on this axis (usually at $\xi = 0$), in the manner of Fig. 2.4.

Suboptimum systems may be handled in the same fashion. If $G_n(\mathbf{V})$ is a test statistic (such that $G_n(\mathbf{V}) \geq 0$), representing a suboptimum detector where $\Lambda_n(\mathbf{V})$ is optimal (in the above Bayes sense), we may then set

$$y = \log G_n(\mathbf{V}) = T_{R\text{-subopt}}^{(N)}\{\mathbf{V}\} \tag{2.37}$$

and write the associated error probabilities as

$$\beta_1^{(0)} = \int_{\log \mathcal{K}_{01}}^{\infty} p_n^{(0)}(y)\, dy \qquad \beta_0^{(1)} = \int_{-\infty}^{\log \mathcal{K}_{01}} p_n^{(1)}(y)\, dy \tag{2.38}$$

The decision process itself is given once more by (2.27) but now with $\log \Lambda_n$ is replaced by $\log G_n$ and the optimum decision rules $\delta_{0,1}^*$ by the suboptimum rules $\delta_{0,1}$. The $p_n^{(0),(1)}$ are the d.d.'s of y under hypotheses H_0: N and H_1: $S \oplus N$, and may be found from Eqs. (2.34) and (2.35) with $x = \log \Lambda_n$ replaced by $y = \log G_n$ therein. The error probabilities $\beta_1^{(0)}$, $\beta_0^{(1)}$ may be represented by Eqs. (2.36), with $F_x^{(0),(1)}(i\xi)$ replaced by $F_y^{(0),(1)}(i\xi)$, the corresponding characteristic functions of y;

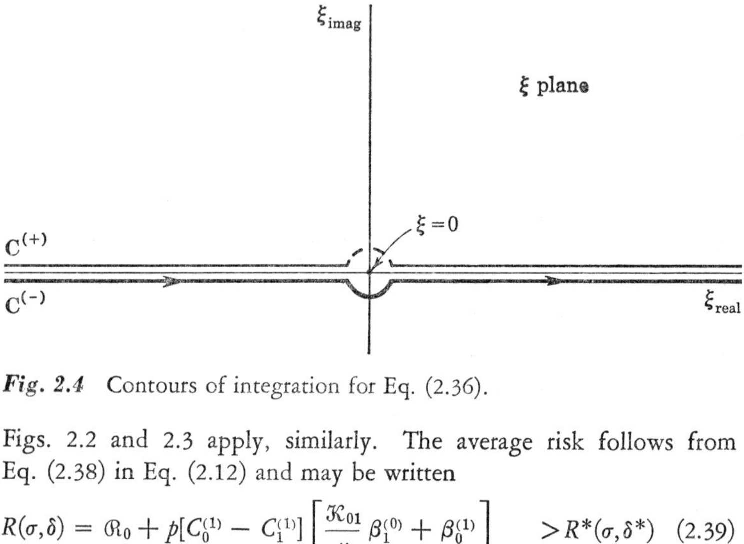

Fig. 2.4 Contours of integration for Eq. (2.36).

Figs. 2.2 and 2.3 apply, similarly. The average risk follows from Eq. (2.38) in Eq. (2.12) and may be written

$$R(\sigma,\delta) = \mathcal{R}_0 + p[C_0^{(1)} - C_1^{(1)}]\left[\frac{\mathcal{K}_{01}}{\mu}\beta_1^{(0)} + \beta_0^{(1)}\right] \qquad > R^*(\sigma,\delta^*) \tag{2.39}$$

analogous to Eq. (2.26). Since these systems are not optimum, they yield a larger average risk, or cost.

Comparisons between optimum and suboptimum detectors, each operating under the same cost assignments, signal and noise environment, and prior probabilities, can now be effected in a variety of ways. One way is to determine for the same average risks and sample sizes the reduction in *input* signal strength† obtained by using the optimum

† Usually normalized in terms of the background noise level, and in this sense an input signal-to-noise ratio.

system x [Eq. (2.32)], instead of the particular suboptimum y; cf. Eq. (2.37). Another is to measure the reduction in average cost, for the *same* input signal level, that is achieved by the optimum detector. Still another may be given by the increase in sample size (observation time) required of the suboptimum device, operating on the same input signals and noise and yielding the same average risk. In some cases it may be convenient to compare systems on the basis of the probabilities of correct decisions, as functions of input signal-to-noise ratio, sample

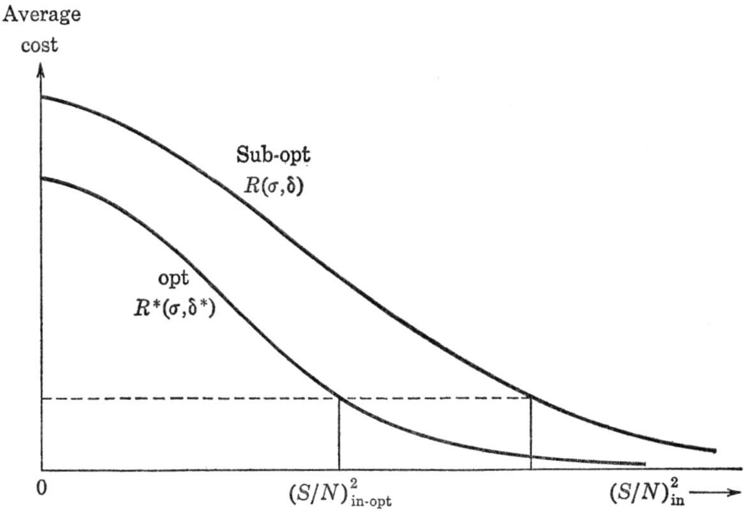

Fig. 2.5 Comparison of an optimum and suboptimum detector: $(S/N)_{\text{in-opt}}$ versus $(S/N)_{\text{in-subopt}}$.

size, and so on. Still other modes of comparison may be found, ultimately dependent upon the associated error probabilities and the signal and noise parameters.† Figure 2.5 shows a typical comparison based on input signal-to-noise ratios.

For the important communication problem of binary signal detection we have, with the help of decision-theory methods, obtained an explicit apparatus for specifying, evaluating, and comparing optimum and suboptimum systems $T_{R\text{-det}}$ for this purpose. Let us now take the final and essential step of determining explicit results for specific examples.

† Ref. 1, sec. 19.3-2.

2.5 *A Simple Example:*† *Coherent Detection*

To illustrate our general remarks of the preceding section we consider the simple but nontrivial example of the optimum (binary) detection of a completely known signal $S(t - \epsilon_0; \theta_0)$ in an additive, normal, random noise background.‡ Detection is thus a test of simple hypotheses with a signal class consisting of but one member (Sec. 2.1). Our problem here is: (1) to determine whether or not the signal, completely specified at the receiver, is present in the noise when a sample of data $\mathbf{V}$ obtained during an interval $(0,T)$, is available; (2) to find the optimum receiver $(\boldsymbol{T}_{R\text{-opt}}^{(N)})$ for this purpose; and (3) to evaluate the expected performance, by calculating the probabilities of decision error (or equivalently, correct decisions) and hence determining the corresponding Bayes risk.

First, we form the likelihood ratio (2.23). It is convenient to use the normalized forms $\mathbf{v} = \mathbf{V}/\sqrt{\psi}$, $\mathbf{k}_N = \mathbf{K}_N/\psi$; $\psi = \overline{N^2}$ $(\overline{N} = 0$, i.e., zero average noise level) (cf. the Appendix) and observe that

$$F_n(\mathbf{V}|\mathbf{0}) = W_n(\mathbf{V})_N = \frac{e^{-\frac{1}{2}\tilde{\mathbf{v}}\mathbf{k}_N^{-1}\mathbf{v}}}{(2\pi)^{n/2}\sqrt{\det(\psi\mathbf{k}_N)}} \tag{2.40}$$

where $W_n(\mathbf{V})_N$ is the n-fold joint d.d. of $\mathbf{V} = \mathbf{N}$, the noise background. Similarly, one finds for the additive signal and noise here that

$$F_n(\mathbf{V}|\mathbf{S}) = W_n(\mathbf{V} - \mathbf{S})_N = \frac{e^{-\frac{1}{2}(\tilde{\mathbf{v}} - a_0\tilde{\mathbf{s}})\mathbf{k}_N^{-1}(\mathbf{v} - a_0\mathbf{s})}}{(2\pi)^{n/2}\sqrt{\det(\psi\mathbf{k}_N)}} \tag{2.41}$$

The known signal $\mathbf{S}$ is normalized according to

$$\mathbf{S} = \frac{A_0}{\sqrt{2}}\,\mathbf{s} = a_0\sqrt{\psi}\mathbf{s} \qquad a_0 \equiv A_0/\sqrt{2\psi} \tag{2.42}$$

with A_0 a "peak" amplitude and a_0^2 the *input signal-to-noise* (power) *ratio*. The desired likelihood ratio (2.23) then follows at once from the ratio of Eq. (2.41) to (2.40). However, for the optimum receiver here we shall use the simpler form $\log \Lambda_n$ [cf. Eqs. (2.27), (2.32)], which is specifically

$$x = \boldsymbol{T}_{R\text{-opt}}^{(N)}\{\mathbf{V}\} = \log \mu - \frac{a_0^2}{2}\Phi_s + a_0\Phi_v \tag{2.43}$$

† Ref. 1, sec. 20.4-1.
‡ See the Appendix for analytical details.

with $\Phi_v \equiv \tilde{\mathbf{v}}\mathbf{k}_N^{-1}\mathbf{s}$ embodying the specific receiver structure, namely, the operations on the received data $\mathbf{V}$, and $\Phi_s \equiv \tilde{\mathbf{s}}\mathbf{k}_N^{-1}\mathbf{s}$ representing a quantity which, as we shall see below [cf. Eq. (2.48)], is defined as (twice) a *processing gain*. The first two terms of Eq. (2.43) constitute a *bias*, since they modify the threshold only and are independent of $\mathbf{v}$. Our optimum test for the presence of this completely known signal is therefore from Eq. (2.43) in (2.27)

Decide

$$H_1\text{: signal (and noise)} \qquad \text{if } a_0\Phi_v \geq \log\,(\mathcal{K}_{01}/\mu) + \frac{a_0^2}{2}\,\Phi_s$$

Decide

$$H_0\text{: noise alone} \qquad \text{if } a_0\Phi_v < \log\,(\mathcal{K}_{01}/\mu) + \frac{a_0^2}{2}\,\Phi_s \tag{2.44}$$

Letting $\tilde{\mathbf{s}}\mathbf{k}_N^{-1} \equiv \tilde{\mathbf{s}}'$ be a weighted signal vector, we see that

$$\Phi_v \equiv \tilde{\mathbf{s}}\mathbf{k}_N^{-1}\mathbf{v} = \tilde{\mathbf{s}}'\mathbf{v} = \sum_i^n s_i'v_i$$

explicitly, so that the optimum receiver structure here requires the (discrete) *cross correlation of the received data element* v_i *with the preset signal components* s_i'. Reception itself is *coherent*, since the signal, and hence its epoch ϵ_0, is known at the detector; cf. Sec. 1.2. The main thing to note is that x, Eq. (2.43), is a *linear* operator on the received data. We shall pursue the question of the interpretation of receiver structure in more detail in Chap. 4.

The characteristic functions and d.d.'s of x, Eq. (2.43), are readily found† from Eqs. (2.40) and (2.41) applied to Eqs. (2.34) and (2.35) to be

$$F_x^{(0),(1)}(i\xi) = \exp\left[-\tfrac{1}{2}a_0^2\Phi_s\xi^2 + i\xi\left(\log\mu \mp \frac{a_0^2}{2}\,\Phi_s\right)\right] \tag{2.45}$$

$$P_n^{(0),(1)}(x) = (2\pi a_0^2\Phi_s)^{-1/2}\exp\left[-(x - \log\mu \pm a_0^2\Phi_s/2)^2/2a_0^2\Phi_s\right] \tag{2.46}$$

where the upper sign refers to H_0, the lower to H_1. The associated error probabilities (2.33) [or (2.36)] become, respectively,

$$\beta_1^{(0)*},\ \beta_0^{(1)*} = \tfrac{1}{2}\left\{1 - \Theta\left[\frac{a_0\sqrt{\Phi_s^{1/2}}}{2\sqrt{2}} \pm \frac{\log\left(\dfrac{\mathcal{K}_{01}}{\mu}\right)}{\sqrt{2}\,a_0\Phi_s^{1/2}}\right]\right\} \tag{2.47}$$

† With the help of eq. (7.26) in Ref. 1.

and the Bayes risk from Eq. (2.47) in Eq. (2.26). Here $\Theta(z) \equiv \frac{2}{\sqrt{\pi}} \int_0^z e^{-t^2}\, dt$ is the familiar error integral.[1] Figure 2.6 shows the type 2 error probability $\beta_0^{(1)*}$ versus the type 1 error probability $\beta_1^{(0)*}$.

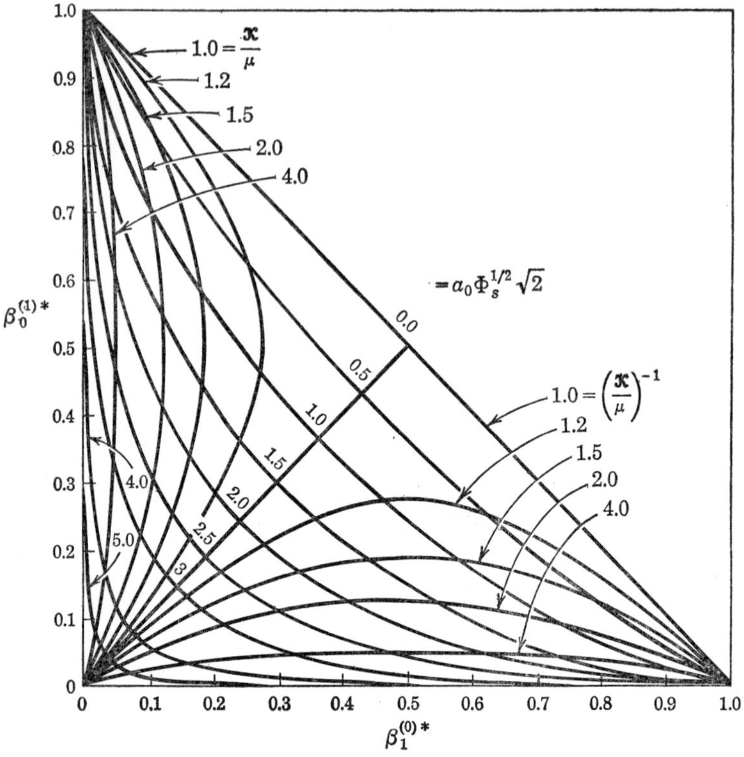

Fig. 2.6 $\beta_0^{(1)*}$ versus $\beta_1^{(0)*}$ for optimum binary detection of a known signal in additive normal noise.

Performance, as exhibited by R^* and the error probabilities, is a canonical function of $a_0^2\Phi_s/2$. In fact, we may define $a_0^2\Phi_s/2$ as the *output* signal-to-noise (power) ratio

$$\left(\frac{S}{N}\right)^2_{\text{out}} \equiv \sigma_0^2 \equiv a_0^2\Phi_s/2 \tag{2.48}$$

or

$$\left(\frac{S}{N}\right)^2_{\text{out}} = \left(\frac{S}{N}\right)^2_{\text{in}} (\Phi_s/2) \tag{2.48a}$$

where $\Phi_s/2$ is the *processing gain* (essentially proportional to sample size n). Note that when the processing gain becomes infinite (with $a_0 > 0$), the error probabilities (2.47) vanish, and detection is perfectly achieved. With finite processing gain and infinite input signal level ($a_0 \to \infty$), a similar result is obtained: perfect detection for $(S/N)^2_{\text{out}} \to \infty$. All this is, of course, entirely consistent with our expectations: if the noise is effectively negligible, the signal, when present, must be unambiguously observable in the received data. On the other hand, if $(S/N)^2_{\text{out}}$ vanishes, the error probabilities may take the values 0, ½, or 1, depending on $\log\left(\frac{\mathcal{K}_{01}}{\mu_{01}}\right)$. In the common communication situation where $\mathcal{K}_{01}/\mu = 1$, we see that then

$$\beta_1^{(0)*} = \beta_0^{(1)*} = \tfrac{1}{2}$$

so that $\frac{\mathcal{K}_{01}}{\mu}\beta_1^{(0)*} + \beta_0^{(1)*} = 1$, and the Bayes risk is not unexpectedly a maximum.

The Neyman-Pearson and Ideal observers [cf. Eqs. (2.29) and (2.30)] are readily found by suitable specialization of Eq. (2.47). Thus, for the former $\beta_1^{(0)}(= \beta_1^{(0)*})$ is fixed, determining a threshold $\mathcal{K}'$ [namely, $\mathcal{K}_{01}$ in Eq. (2.47)], and so we have

$$\beta_0^{(1)*} \to \beta_{0-NP}^{(1)*} = \tfrac{1}{2}\left\{1 - \Theta\left[\frac{\sigma_0}{2} - \frac{\log(\mathcal{K}'/\mu)}{2\sigma_0}\right]\right\} \tag{2.49a}$$

and

$$\log \mathcal{K}' = \log \mu + 2\sigma_0\Theta^{-1}[1 - 2\beta_1^{(0)}] - \sigma_0^2 \tag{2.49b}$$

with

$$\beta_0^{(1)*} = \tfrac{1}{2}\{1 - \Theta[\sigma_0 - \Theta^{-1}(1 - 2\beta_1^{(0)})]\} \tag{2.49c}$$

where Θ^{-1} is the inverse error integral. For the Ideal Observer the error probabilities are again given by Eq. (2.47), where $\mathcal{K}_{01}(= \mathcal{K}_I)$ is set equal to unity. The optimum receiver in both instances is still the linear operator on $\mathbf{v}$ indicated in Eq. (2.43).

Our model so far has considered only discrete sampling in time on the observation interval $(0,T)$, where n is the number of data samples $[v_i = v(t_i),\ i = 1, \ldots, n]$ received in that interval. The theory is directly extended to include continuous sampling. Instead of a likelihood ratio (or its logarithm) as optimum detector, we now have the logarithm of the likelihood-ratio *functional*, $\log \Lambda_T(V(t))$, which is, from Eq. (2.43), specifically

$$x_T = \log \Lambda_T(V(t)) = \log \mu - \frac{a_0^2}{2}(\Phi_T)_s + a_0(\Phi_T)_v \qquad (2.50)$$

where now

$$(\Phi_T)_s = \psi \int_{0-}^{T+} s(t - \epsilon_0, \boldsymbol{\theta}_0) X_T(t;\epsilon_0,\boldsymbol{\theta}_0)\, dt \qquad (2.51a)$$

$$(\Phi_T)_v = \psi \int_{0-}^{T+} v(t) X_T(t;\epsilon,\boldsymbol{\theta}_0)\, dt \qquad V(t) = v(t)\sqrt{\psi} \qquad (2.51b)$$

which are discussed in the Appendix. Here ϵ_0 is a known signal epoch characteristic of coherent reception (cf. Fig. 1.2 and discussion in Sec. 1.2); $\boldsymbol{\theta}_0$ represent other parameters of the (normalized) signal waveform $s = \sqrt{2}\, S(t - \epsilon_0, \boldsymbol{\theta}_0)/A_0$ [cf. Eq. (2.42)], while X_T is, in fact, the weighting function† of a linear filter $X_T = h_T(T - t)$ (cf. Chap. 4, Sec. 4.2).

The decision process is described again by (2.44), with x replaced by x_T [Eq. (2.50)] therein. The d.d.'s and characteristic functions of $\mathbf{x}_T$, the associated error probabilities, and output signal-to-noise ratios and processing gain are likewise given by Eqs. (2.45) to (2.48*a*), with $(\Phi_T)_s$, $(\Phi_T)_v$ in place of Φ_s, Φ_v, of course, while Fig. 2.6 remains unchanged, subject only to these modifications.

A limiting case of considerable interest in applications occurs when the background noise is "white," i.e., has a uniform intensity spectrum for all frequencies and a (nonzero) spectral intensity density‡ W_0. The optimum detector here (for continuous sampling only) is found to be

$$x_T \Big|_{\text{white}} = \log \mu - \frac{A_0^2}{2W_0} \int_0^T s(t - \epsilon_0, \boldsymbol{\theta}_0)^2\, dt + \frac{A_0\sqrt{2}}{W_0} \int_0^T V(t) s(t - \epsilon_0, \boldsymbol{\theta})\, dt \qquad (2.52)$$

showing once more that the *optimum structure requires the cross correlation of the received wave $V(t)$ with the known, locally generated signal waveform* $s(t - \epsilon_0, \boldsymbol{\theta})$ [or $S(t - \epsilon_0, \boldsymbol{\theta}) = \frac{A_0}{\sqrt{2}} s(t - \epsilon_0, \boldsymbol{\theta})$]. The output signal-

† The weighting X_T is obtained as the solution of a certain integral equation whose kernel is the covariance function $K_N(t,u)$ of the background-noise process; cf. (A.7).

‡ Ref. 1, pp. 146, 148, 352, and 353.

to-noise ratio (2.48) is now

$$\left(\frac{S}{N}\right)^2_{\text{out-white}} = \frac{a_0^2}{2}(\Phi_T)_s\Big|_{\text{white}} = \frac{A_0^2}{2W_0}\int_0^T s(t-\epsilon_0,\theta_0)^2\,dt = \frac{E_s}{W_0} \tag{2.53}$$

where E_s is the received signal energy. Thus, the output signal-to-noise ratio (2.53) represents the total effective *signal energy* received against *effective noise power per cycle* (or per unit bandwidth).

Note that if we let B'_e be an effective signal bandwidth [namely, the spectral width(s) of the region(s) where the signal spectrum is essentially nonvanishing], we may write $\overline{N_{\text{in}}^2} = B'_e W_0$ and $\overline{S_{\text{in}}^2} = E_s/T$, so that Eq. (2.53) becomes alternatively

$$\left(\frac{S}{N}\right)^2_{\text{out-white}} = \frac{E_s}{W_0} = \left(\frac{E_s}{TW_0B'_e}\right)(TB'_e) = \left(\frac{S}{N}\right)^2_{\text{in-white}} \cdot TB'_e \tag{2.54}$$

By comparison with Eq. (2.48*a*) we may call the effective time-bandwidth product TB'_e the processing gain here. Similarly, for general, nonwhite noise we can define an effective signal bandwidth B_e, such that

$$B_eT \equiv (\Phi_T)_s/2 \tag{2.55}$$

which shows once more [cf. (2.48)] that

$$(S/N)^2_{\text{out}} = a_0^2(\Phi_T)_s/2 = (S/N)^2_{\text{in}}B_eT$$

with B_eT the processing gain. In general, the larger the processing gain, the smaller the probabilities of error and the Bayes risk. We have seen this specifically in the above example, through Eq. (2.47).

2.6 *Extensions: Incoherent Detection*

The simple model of the preceding section can be extended to more general situations, which fit more closely the usual communication environment. Two important situations for which exact results (at all input signal levels) can be obtained are (1) the incoherent detection of narrow-band deterministic signals in additive normal noise and (2) the same model as (1) but now subject to slow Rayleigh fading of the signal amplitudes. The signals in (1) are assumed completely specified at the receiver except for RF epoch ϵ [cf. Eq. (2.56)], while for case (2) signal amplitude is also not known—only the rms value ($\sim\sqrt{\overline{a_0^2}}$) is given as a measure of the fading. Case (1) is appropriate for some radar applications, and case (2) is often encountered in the communications environment. For the narrow-band signals considered here we can write, again in normalized form [cf. Eq. (2.42)],

$$s(t-\epsilon;\boldsymbol{\theta}_0) = F_s(t;\boldsymbol{\theta}_0)\cos[\omega_0(t-\epsilon)-\varphi_s(t;\boldsymbol{\theta}_0)] \tag{2.56}$$

where $\boldsymbol{\theta}_0$ is a set of known signal parameters, F_s and φ_s are an envelope and phase, and ω_0 is the (angular) carrier frequency of the normalized signal $s(t-\epsilon;\boldsymbol{\theta}_0)$.

For case (1) with continuous sampling on an interval $(0,T)$ the optimum detector is found to be†

$$y = T_R^{(N)}\{V(t)\} = \log\mu - \frac{a_0^2}{2}B_T + \log I_0(a_0\sqrt{\Psi_0}) \tag{2.57}$$

where

$$B_T = \frac{\psi}{2}\int_{-\infty}^{\infty}[a(t;\boldsymbol{\theta}_0)X_T(t;\boldsymbol{\theta}_0)_0 + b(t;\boldsymbol{\theta}_0)Y_T(t;\boldsymbol{\theta}_0)]\,dt$$

with

$$\begin{aligned} a(t;\boldsymbol{\theta}_0) &= F_s\cos(\omega_0 t-\varphi_s) \\ b(t;\boldsymbol{\theta}_0) &= F_s\sin(\omega_0 t-\varphi_s) \end{aligned} \tag{2.58a}$$

$$\Psi_0 = \psi^2\iint_{-\infty}^{\infty} v(t)D_T(t,u;\boldsymbol{\theta}_0)_0 v(u)\,dt\,du \tag{2.58b}$$

in which

$$\begin{aligned} D_T(t,u;\boldsymbol{\theta}_0)_0 &= X_T(t;\boldsymbol{\theta}_0)_0X_T(u;\boldsymbol{\theta}_0)_0 + Y_T(t;\boldsymbol{\theta}_0)_0Y_T(u;\boldsymbol{\theta}_0)_0 \qquad -0 < t,\, u < T+ \\ &= 0 \qquad \text{elsewhere} \end{aligned} \tag{2.58c}$$

and $X_{T,0}$, $Y_{T,0}$ are the solutions of a pair of integral equations, again with the noise covariance function $K_N(t,u)$ as kernel [cf. the Appendix and Eq. (A.10) therein]. Since y is monotonic in $a_0^2\Psi_0$, an equivalent but much simpler optimum structure is

$$z = T_R^{(N)\prime}\{V(t)\} = a_0^2\Psi_0(V(t)) \tag{2.59}$$

Now instead of comparing y against the threshold $\log\mathcal{K}$, we observe that the optimum test (2.27) becomes

$$\begin{aligned} &\text{Decide} \\ &H_1\text{: signal and noise} \qquad \text{if } z = a_0^2\Psi_0 \geq K_T \\ &\text{Decide} \\ &H_0\text{: noise alone} \qquad \text{if } z = a_0^2\Psi_0 < K_T \end{aligned} \tag{2.60}$$

† Ref. 1, secs. 20.1-3 and 20.2-3.

where $K_T(\geq 0)$ is the solution of

$$\log I_0(\sqrt{K_T}) = \log (\mathcal{K}/\mu) + (a_0^2/2)B_T$$

[from Eq. (2.59) in Eq. (2.57)]; cf. (2.44). Note from Eq. (2.58*b*) that out optimum detector is now a *nonlinear* operator on the received data $V(t)$. In fact, as we shall see in more detail in Chap. 4, Ψ_0 basically involves an averaged *autocorrelation* of the received data with itself, characteristic of incoherent detection processes.†

The characteristic functions (2.35) and d.d.'s (2.34) of the test functions z, and the associated Bayes error probabilities [Eqs. (2.33) and (2.36)], have been found to be[4,5]

$$F_z(i\xi|H_0) = (1 - 4i\xi\sigma^2)^{-1} \qquad F_z(i\xi|H_1) = \frac{e^{\frac{4\sigma^4 i\xi}{1-4i\xi\sigma^2}}}{1 - 4i\xi\sigma^2} \tag{2.61}$$

$$\begin{aligned} w_1(z|H_0) &= \frac{e^{-z/4\sigma^2}}{4\sigma^2} \quad z > 0 \qquad & w_1(z|H_1) &= \frac{e^{-\sigma^2 - z/4\sigma^2}}{4\sigma^2} I_0(\sqrt{z}) \quad z > 0 \\ &= 0 \quad z < 0 & &= 0 \quad z < 0 \end{aligned} \tag{2.62}$$

and

$$\begin{aligned} \beta_1^{(0)*} = e^{-K_T/4\sigma^2} \quad K_T \geq 0 \qquad \beta_0^{(1)*} &= 1 - Q(\sigma\sqrt{2}; \sqrt{K_T}/\sigma\sqrt{2}) \\ &= 1 - Q(\sigma\sqrt{2}; \sqrt{-2\log \beta_1^{(0)*}}) \end{aligned} \tag{2.63}$$

Here $Q(\alpha{:}\beta) \equiv \int_\beta^\infty e^{-\alpha^2/2-\lambda^2/2}\lambda I_0(\alpha\lambda)\,d\lambda$ is the so-called "Q function" [cf. Eq. (A.17) et seq.], and σ^2 is defined as the output signal-to-noise ratio

$$\sigma^2 = \frac{a_0^2}{2} B_T \equiv \left(\frac{S}{N}\right)^2_{\text{out}} \tag{2.64}$$

From this we see that $B_T/2$, like $\Phi_s/2$ in the coherent example of Sec. 2.5, is a processing gain and hence, by an argument similar to that leading to Eq. (2.55), is equal to $B_e'T$, the effective time-bandwidth product of the processed signal.

Figures 2.7*A* and *B* show the d.d.'s [Eqs. (2.62)] of z and the associated error probabilities‡ [Eqs. (2.63)]. As expected, the error probabilities

† See Eqs. (2.79) and comments.
‡ Note that the threshold K_T is a function of σ^2. For small and large values of K_T one has $K_T = 4(\log \mathcal{K}/\mu + \sigma^2)$, $K_T \simeq (\log \mathcal{K}/\mu + \sigma^2)^2$, respectively. For example, if $\mathcal{K}/\mu = 1$, it follows from Eqs. (2.63) that $\beta_1^{(0)*} \to e^{-1}$, $\beta_0^{(1)*} \to 1 - e^{-1}$ $(\sigma \to 0)$, and that $\beta_1^{(0)*} \simeq e^{-\sigma^2/4}$, $\beta_0^{(1)*} \simeq 1 - Q(\sigma\sqrt{2}; \mathcal{K}/\sqrt{2}) \to 0$, as $\sigma^2 \to \infty$.

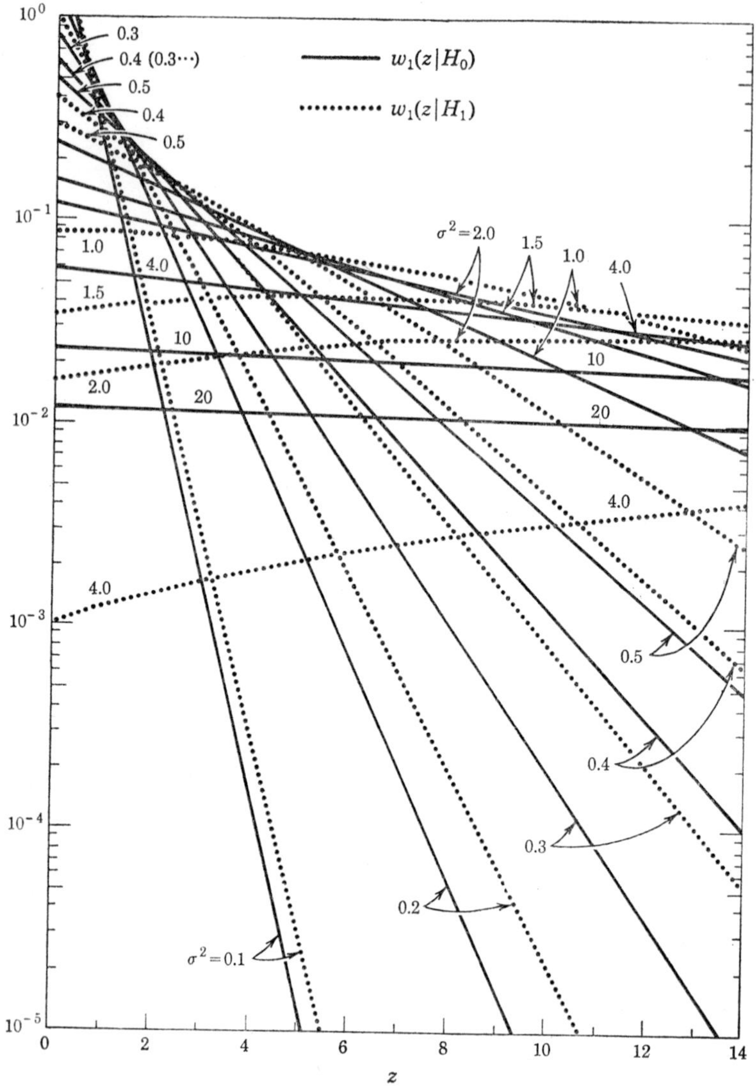

Fig. 2.7A Case (1): The d.d.'s of z [Eq. (2.59)], the optimum detector structure.

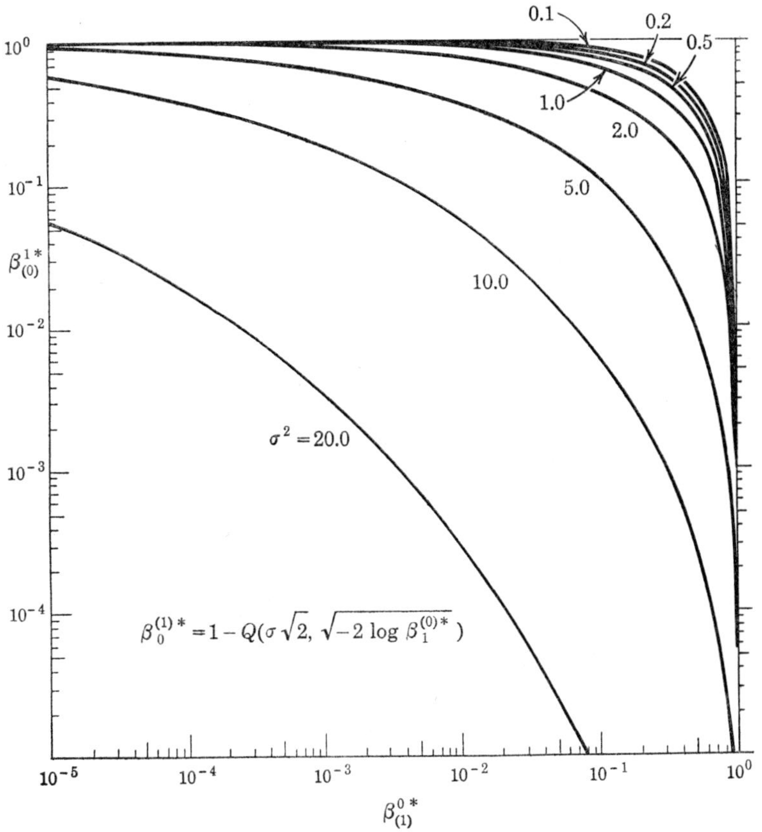

Fig. 2.7B Case (1): Error probabilities for incoherent detection of narrow-band deterministic signals of known amplitude.

vanish as the output signal-to-noise ratio becomes indefinitely large, but when it becomes vanishingly small, $\beta_1^{(0)*}$, $\beta_0^{(1)*}$ are different from ½, in contrast to the coherent case of the previous example (cf. Fig. 2.6 for $\mathcal{K}/\mu = 1$), a result that stems from the nongaussian nature of the detector characteristic, or test statistic z: cf. Eq. (2.60).

Case (2), where the signal amplitude is subject to slow Rayleigh fading, is handled in a similar way. The optimum structure here is found to be,[4] again for continuous sampling on $(0,T)$,

$$y_R = T_R^{(N)}\{V(t)\} = \log \mu - \log (1 + \sigma_R^2) + \frac{\overline{a_0^2}\Psi_0}{4(1 + \sigma_R^2)} \tag{2.65}$$

where now the output signal-to-noise ratio (2.64) is modified to $\sigma_R^2 = \overline{a_0^2} B_T/2$. Although the structure y_R is proportional to Ψ_0, as is z above for the fixed-amplitude situation, the characteristic functions and d.d.'s of y_R are different, because of the Rayleigh fading, and so, consequently, are the error probabilities. These quantities are[4]

$$F_{y_R}(i\xi|H_0) = \frac{e^{i\xi A_T}}{1 - i\xi\sigma_R^2/(1+\sigma_R^2)} \qquad F_{y_R}(i\xi|H_1) = \frac{e^{i\xi A_T}}{1 - i\xi\sigma_R^2} \tag{2.66a}$$

$$w_1(y_R|H_0) = \frac{e^{-(y_R - A_T)(1+\sigma_R^2)/\sigma_R^2}}{\sigma_R^2/(1+\sigma_R^2)} \qquad y_R > A_T$$

$$w_1(y_R|H_1) = \frac{e^{-(y_R - A_T)/\sigma_R^2}}{\sigma_R^2} \qquad y_R > A_T \tag{2.66b}$$

with

$$A_T = \log \mu - \log(1 + \sigma_R^2)$$

and

$$\left.\begin{aligned} \beta_1^{(0)*} &= e^{-\lambda_0(\sigma_R^2+1)/\sigma_R^2} && \lambda_0 \geq 0 \\ &= 1 && \lambda_0 \leq 0 \\ \beta_0^{(1)*} &= 1 - e^{-\lambda_0/\sigma_R^2} = 1 - e^{(\log \beta_1^{(0)*})/(1+\sigma_R^2)} && \lambda_0 \geq 0 \\ &= 0 && \lambda_0 \leq 0 \end{aligned}\right\} \begin{aligned} \lambda_0 &= \log \frac{\mathcal{K}}{\mu} \\ &+ \log(1+\sigma_R^2) \end{aligned} \tag{2.67}$$

The d.d.'s [Eqs. (2.66)] and the error probabilities [Eqs. (2.67)] are shown in Figs. 2.8*A* and *B* for some typical values of σ_R^2 as parameter.

Although the optimum detector structure has the same form here as in case (1), except for a preset scale factor, the error probabilities behave differently as a function of output signal-to-noise ratio, because of fading. However, the error probabilities still vanish as $\sigma_R^2 \to \infty$, as expected [cf. Eqs. (2.67)], while for indefinitely weak signals ($\sigma_R^2 \to 0$) we note that $\beta_1^{(0)*} = 1, e^{-1}, 0$, and $\beta_0^{(1)*} = 0, 1 - e^{-1}, 1$ when $\log \mathcal{K}/\mu < 0, = 0, > 0$, respectively [which is the same behavior as case (1), for $\mathcal{K}/\mu = 0$].

In the important situation of white noise backgrounds we easily find† that the optimum detectors z, y_R [Eqs. (2.59) and (2.65)] become

$$z\Big|_{\text{white}} = \frac{2A_0^2}{W_0^2}\left|\int_0^T V(t)F_s(t)e^{i[\omega_0 t - \varphi_s(t)]}\,dt\right|^2 \tag{2.68}$$

and

$$y_R\Big|_{\text{white}} = \log \mu - \log(1+\sigma_R^2) + \frac{\overline{A_0^2}}{2W_0^2(1+\sigma_R^2)}\left|\int_0^T V(t)F_s(t)e^{i(\omega_0 t - \varphi_s)}\,dt\right|^2 \tag{2.69}$$

† Ref. 1, p. 863. See also the Appendix of the present monograph.

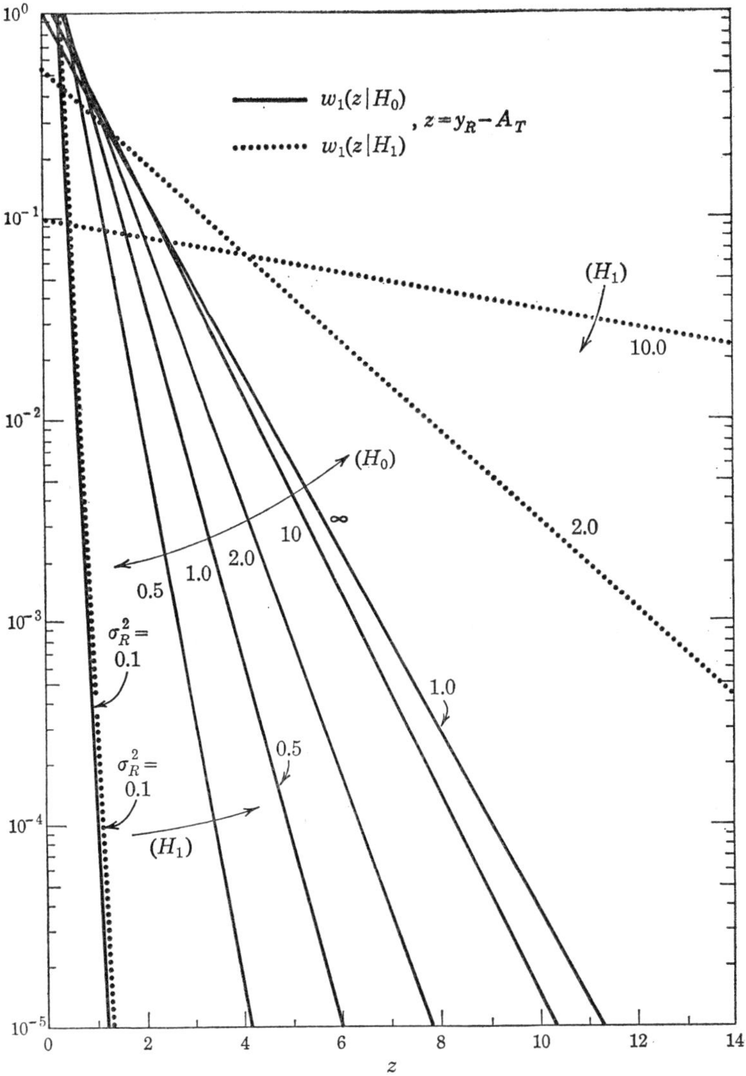

Fig. 2.8A Case (2): Rayleigh fading. The d.d.'s of y_R [Eq. (2.65)].

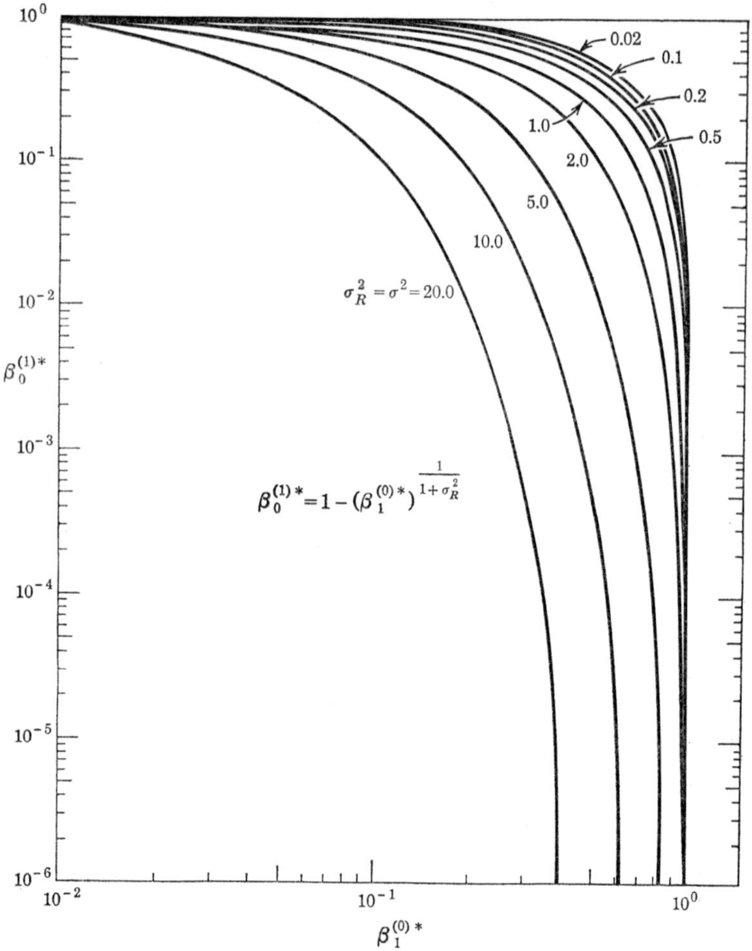

Fig. 2.8B Case (2). Error probabilities for incoherent detection of narrow-band deterministic signals with Rayleigh fading.

and the output signal-to-noise ratios σ^2, σ_R^2 are now [cf. Eqs. (2.64) and (2.65)]

$$\sigma^2\Big|_{\text{white}} = \frac{A_0^2}{4W_0}\int_0^T F_s^2(t,\theta_0)\,dt = \frac{E_s}{W_0} \qquad E_s = \frac{A_0^2}{4}\int_0^T F_s^2(t,\theta)\,dt \tag{2.70}$$

[cf. Eqs. (2.53)] and

$$\sigma_R^2\Big|_{\text{white}} = \overline{\sigma^2}\Big|_{\text{white}} = \bar{E}_s/W_0 \tag{2.71}$$

where the average is over the amplitude A_0. Again, with white noise backgrounds the output signal-to-noise ratio may be equivalently interpreted as a ratio of total (average) signal energy to noise intensity density, as in the coherent cases discussed earlier [cf. Eqs. (2.53) to (2.55)]. Alternatively, we may define processing gain here with the help of Eq. (2.54) in Eqs. (2.70) and (2.71).

2.7 *Some Canonical Results*

The examples above, although important in their own right, are rather special in that *exact* expressions for the detection probabilities can be obtained. This is not possible generally, since $\log \Lambda(\mathbf{V})$, $\log \Lambda_T(V)$ are themselves not expressible in closed form. The theory fortunately can still be used in most applications; however, if we observe that (1) optimization for *threshold operation*† is (with care) sufficient to ensure good (i.e., absolutely *better*) performance at stronger signal levels, where optimality is no longer a primary concern, and (2) that explicit forms of the optimum detector structure ($\log \Lambda$) may be obtained by a suitable expansion‡ in terms of the input signal-to-noise ratio a_0.

Such an expansion may be justified in terms of the notion of *local optimality*.[6,7] Specifically, we define[7] a *locally optimum detector as one which has the same average risk and the same derivative of the average risk as the Bayes detector when* $a_0 = 0$. Letting θ represent a measure of the input signal-to-noise ratio a_0^2, we see that our definition of local optimality here becomes

$$\hat{R}(\theta,\hat{\delta})_{\theta=0} = R^*(\theta;\delta^*)_{\theta=0} \qquad \frac{\partial \hat{R}}{\partial \theta}\Big|_{\theta=0} = \frac{\partial R^*}{\partial \theta}\Big|_{\theta=0} \tag{2.72}$$

† By *threshold operation* is meant reception with *weak* input signal-to-noise ratios ($a_0^2 \ll 1$), but with sufficient processing gain so that ($a_0^2B_T/2 =$) $a_0^2B_eT \gg 1$, which is the usual limiting condition of system operation; cf. Eqs. (2.55) and (2.64).

‡ Ref. 1, sec. 19.4.

where $\hat{\delta}$ and δ^* are respectively the locally optimum and Bayes decision rules. Expressed variationally, the condition (2.72) becomes

$$\left\{\min_{\delta \to \hat{\delta}} \left[\frac{\partial R(\theta,\delta)}{\partial \theta} + \lambda R(\theta,\delta)\right]\right\}_{\theta=0} = \hat{I}(\geq 0) \tag{2.72a}$$

With the help of Eq. (2.72) in Eq. (2.72*a*) we find that the appropriate decision rules $\delta_{1,0}$ are here

Decide

$$\gamma_1; H_1 \quad \text{if} \left(\frac{\partial}{\partial \theta} \log \Lambda_n\right)_{\theta=0} \geq \lambda\left(\frac{\mathcal{K}}{\mu} - 1\right) \quad \text{with } \hat{\delta}_1 = 1$$

and
decide (2.73)

$$\gamma_0; H_0 \quad \text{if} \left(\frac{\partial}{\partial \theta} \log \Lambda_n\right)_{\theta=0} < \lambda\left(\frac{\mathcal{K}}{\mu} - 1\right) \quad \text{with } \hat{\delta}_0 = 1$$

In the binary, "on-off" cases (H_1: $S \otimes N$; H_0: N) the locally optimum detector structure has the canonical form,[7] *terminating with the term* $0(\theta)$,

$$\hat{x} = \hat{T}_{R\text{-opt}}(\mathbf{V}) = \log \mu + \hat{B}_n(\theta) + \theta\left(\frac{\partial \log \Lambda_n}{\partial \theta}\right)_{\theta=0} \tag{2.74}$$

where the bias $\hat{B}_n(\theta)$ is usually chosen to ensure that the error probabilities $(\hat{\alpha}, \hat{\beta})$ vanish with sufficiently large sample sizes $(n, T \to \infty)$. Furthermore, one can show[7] that $\hat{x}$ is often asymptotically as effective as the exact form $\log \Lambda_n$ in the limit as n(or T) $\to \infty$, in achieving minimum average error probabilities (and Bayes risk).

It can also be shown[7] that for optimum sequential detection [with linear average risk: cf. Eq. (2.31)] the locally optimum detector now has the form

$$\hat{x}_s = \hat{B}_s(\hat{m},\theta) + \theta\left(\frac{\partial \log \Lambda_{\hat{m}}}{\partial \theta}\right)_{\theta=0} \tag{2.74a}$$

As a necessary and sufficient condition for this, log $\Lambda_{\hat{m}}$ *must likewise be linear in sample size as* $\theta \to 0$. The bias $\hat{B}_s$ is chosen to satisfy the conditions

$$\hat{R}_s\Big|_{\theta=0} = R^*_{\text{seq}}\Big|_{\theta=0} \qquad \left(\frac{\partial \hat{R}_s}{\partial \theta}\right)\Big|_{\theta=0} = \left(\frac{\partial R^*_{\text{seq}}}{\partial \theta}\right)\Big|_{\theta=0} \tag{2.74b}$$

analogous to Eq. (2.72) for the fixed sample cases. The test procedure is the same as Eq. (2.31*a*), with x_s replaced by $\hat{x}_s$.

We emphasize that Eq. (2.74) applies for nonnormal as well as normal statistics, for general signal types (which may be stochastic as well as deterministic), for combinations of signal and noise that need not be additive, and for continuous as well as discrete sampling. It can also be shown that in approximating the optimum structure (Λ_n or any monotonic function of Λ_n), *it is the logarithm* ($\log \Lambda_n$) *that is the proper function to develop in a power series in* θ, *and that such a series always terminates with the term* $O(\theta)$; cf. Eqs. (2.32) and (2.34). In terms of an optimality procedure that is Bayes in the limit $\theta = 0$ [cf. Eq. (2.72*a*)] we can thus make precise the intuitive notion† that $\log \Lambda_n$ is the natural structure to approximate by expansion in the input signal-to-noise ratio (θ) and to specify the point at which this expansion must terminate. Expressions of the form (2.74) provide the basis of a quantitive detection theory in most realistic situations.

In the important case of *additive signal and noise processes* one has for the threshold development of the optimum binary structure [$\log \Lambda_n$ above and discrete sampling on $(0,T)$]

$$\log \Lambda_n = \log \mu + \theta \tilde{\mathbf{y}}\bar{\mathbf{s}}' + \frac{\theta^2}{2!}[\tilde{\mathbf{y}}(\boldsymbol{\rho} - \bar{\mathbf{s}}'\bar{\tilde{\mathbf{s}}}')\mathbf{y} + \operatorname{trace} \boldsymbol{\rho}\tilde{\mathbf{z}}] + O(\theta^3) \tag{2.75a}$$

$$\log \Lambda_n = \log \mu + \theta \left(\frac{\partial \log \Lambda_n}{\partial \theta}\right)_0 + \frac{\theta^2}{2!}\left(\frac{\partial^2 \log \Lambda_n}{\partial \theta^2}\right)_0 + O(\theta^3) \tag{2.75b}$$

where‡

$$\mathbf{y} = [y_i] \equiv \left[\frac{-1}{W_0}\frac{\partial W_0}{\partial V_i}\right] \qquad \boldsymbol{\rho} = [\overline{s_i' s_j'}] \equiv \boldsymbol{\rho}_s$$
$$\mathbf{z} = [z_{ij}] \equiv \left[\frac{\partial^2}{\partial V_i\, \partial V_j} \log W_0\right] \tag{2.76}$$

in which $W_0 = W_0(\mathbf{V}) = F_n(\mathbf{V}|\mathbf{0})$ is the n-fold d.d. of the background noise alone; the $V_i = V(t_i)$, $i = 1, \ldots, n$, are the received data samples in $(0,T)$; and $\boldsymbol{\rho}$, $\mathbf{z}$ are $(n \times n)$ matrices, with $\mathbf{y}$ a (column) vector, as indicated. The quantity $\boldsymbol{\rho} - \bar{\mathbf{s}}'\bar{\tilde{\mathbf{s}}}'$ is the autovariance matrix of the (somewhat differently) normalized§ signal $\mathbf{s}'$; cf. Eq. (2.42).

† Ref. 1, sec. 19.4-1.

‡ Equation (2.75*a*) is also the logarithmic expansion of a somewhat generalized form of Rudnick's development (see Ref. 8) and is the *unexpanded* form (in the V_i now) of the author's original canonical threshold detector (Ref. 1, sec. 19.4, and refs. 1 and 21 therein).

§ Here $\mathbf{s}' = a_0\mathbf{s}/\sqrt{\overline{a_0^2}}$, and therefore $\overline{s_i' s_j'} = \overline{s_i s_j} = (\rho_s)_{ij}$ for the more familiar form Eq. (2.42).

The canonical, locally optimum detector (2.74) is accordingly here

$$\hat{x}_{\text{coh}} = \log \mu + \hat{B}_n^{(c)}(\theta_c) + \theta_c \bar{\tilde{\mathbf{y}}}\bar{\mathbf{s}}' \tag{2.77a}$$

$$\hat{x}_{\text{incoh}} = \log \mu + \hat{B}_n^{(I)}(\theta_I) + \frac{\theta_I}{2}[\tilde{\mathbf{y}}\boldsymbol{\varrho}\mathbf{y} + \text{trace}\ \boldsymbol{\varrho}\tilde{\mathbf{z}}] \tag{2.77b}$$

where $\theta_c = \sqrt{\overline{a_0^2}}$ for coherent reception $[\bar{\mathbf{s}}' \neq 0]$ and $\theta_I = \overline{a_0^2}$ for incoherent observation $[\bar{\mathbf{s}}' = \bar{\mathbf{s}} = 0]$, and consequently $\theta_I = \theta_c^2$.

Similar expressions are obtained in the sequential cases; cf. Eq. (2.74*a*). One has instead of Eqs. (2.77)

$$\hat{x}_{\text{s-coh}} = \hat{B}^{(c)}(\hat{m},\theta_c) + \theta_c \hat{\tilde{\mathbf{y}}}\hat{\bar{\mathbf{s}}}' \tag{2.78a}$$

$$\hat{x}_{\text{s-incoh}} = \hat{B}^{(I)}(\hat{m},\theta_I) + \frac{\theta_I}{2}[\hat{\tilde{\mathbf{y}}}\hat{\boldsymbol{\varrho}}\hat{\mathbf{y}} + \text{trace}\ \hat{\boldsymbol{\varrho}}\hat{\tilde{\mathbf{z}}}] \tag{2.78b}$$

Here $\mathbf{y} \to \hat{\mathbf{y}}$, $\mathbf{s}' \to \hat{\bar{\mathbf{s}}}'$, etc., where these vectors and matrices are now of random dimensionality, since sample size $m \to \hat{m}$ is a random variable.

To obtain a still more explicit interpretation of structure in terms of specific operations on the received data $\mathbf{V}$ itself, we now expand $\mathbf{y}$ (or $\hat{\mathbf{y}}$) and $\mathbf{z}$ (or $\hat{\mathbf{z}}$) [Eqs. (2.76)] about $\mathbf{V} = \mathbf{0}$ [in the manner of eqs. (19.42) to (19.45) of Ref. 1], where we write

$$W_0(\mathbf{V}) = \exp B^{(0)} \cdot \exp [\tilde{\mathbf{V}}\mathbf{b}^{(1)} + (\tilde{\mathbf{V}}\mathbf{b}^{(2)})^2 + \cdots] \tag{2.79a}$$

The result is eq. (19.45) of Ref. 1, in which now

$$\begin{aligned} \mathbf{y} &= \sqrt{\psi_N}\,[-\mathbf{b}^{(1)} - 2(\mathbf{b}^{(2)}\tilde{\mathbf{b}}^{(2)})\mathbf{V} - 0(V^2,V^3, \ldots)] \\ \mathbf{z} &= \psi_N[2\mathbf{b}^{(2)}\tilde{\mathbf{b}}^{(2)} + 0(V,V^2)] \end{aligned} \tag{2.79b}$$

From this in Eqs. (2.77*a*) and (2.77*b*) we can say, canonically, that optimum *coherent* threshold detection requires (averaged, weighted) *cross correlations* of the received data with the (averaged) signal waveform, whereas incoherent reception always implies (averaged, weighted) *autocorrelations* of the received data with itself.† Analogous results for sequential detectors, and for continuous sampling, are obtained in the usual way (for the latter cf. sec. 19.4-2 of Ref. 1). We shall consider specific structures in more detail in Chap. 4.

Of course, more than structure is needed to describe performance adequately. We must also determine the error probabilities and Bayes risk, in the manner of Sec. 2.4, where now $\hat{x}$ [Eqs. (2.74) and (2.77)] are the appropriate optimum forms, whose d.d.'s $w_1(\hat{x}|H_{0,1})$ are required.

† Provided $W_0(\mathbf{V})$ is symmetric (about 0) so that $\mathbf{b}^{(1)} = \mathbf{b}^{(3)} = \cdots = 0$, a common case. With W_0 unsymmetrical ($\mathbf{b}^{(1)}$, $\mathbf{b}^{(3)}$, etc., $\neq 0$) one has, in addition, cross correlations as well as autocorrelations in the structure.

No completely general statements are possible here; the results depend strongly on the statistics of the background noise, and evaluation of $w(\hat{x}|H_{0,1})$ is a matter of ingenuity. However, when the background noise is normal and when **y** depends linearly on **V** for the most part, $w(\hat{x}|H_{0,1})$ is normal for coherent observation (cf. Sec. 2.5) and may be asymptotically normal for incoherent observation, provided the correlation function of the signal process has a decay time that is short compared to the observation interval T. An example is provided by gaussian signals in normal noise with sufficiently long observation periods T vis-à-vis (signal bandwidth)$^{-1}$. If the signal process is deterministic and in addition has a correlation function that does not have a sufficiently short decay time, normality no longer applies, and $\hat{x}$ has some form of general, noncentral χ^2 distribution with an effectively *small* number of degrees of freedom. The examples of Sec. 2.6 illustrate this case.

References

1. Middleton, D: "An Introduction to Statistical Communication Theory," McGraw-Hill Book Company, New York, 1960.
2. Ogg, F. C., Jr.: A Note on Bayes Detection of Signals, *IRE, Trans. Inform. Theory*, **IT-10**:57 (1964).
3. Bussgang, J. J., and D. Middleton: Optimum Sequential Detection of Signals in Noise, *IRE, Trans. Inform. Theory*, **IT-1**:5 (1955).
4. Middleton, D.: On the Exact Calculation of Error Probabilities in the Detection of Signals with Coherent Structure, Observed Incoherently in Normal Noise, *Raytheon Co. Res. Div. Tech. Mem.* T-370, December, 1961.
5. Helstrom, C. W.: "Statistical Theory of Signal Detection," p. 150, Pergamon Press, New York, 1960.
6. Capon, J.: On the Asymptotic Efficiency of Locally Optimum Detectors, *IRE, Trans. Inform. Theory*, **IT-7**:67 (1961).
7. Middleton, D.: Canonically Optimum Threshold Detection, *RAND Rept.* (In preparation.)
8. Rudnick, P.: Likelihood Detection of Small Signals in Stationary Noise, *J. Appl. Phys.*, **32**:40 (1961).
9. Davenport, W. B., Jr., and W. L. Root: "Introduction to the Theory of Random Signals and Noise," McGraw-Hill Book Company, New York, 1958.
10. Wainstein, L. A., and V. D. Zubakov: "Extraction of Signals from Noise," trans. by R. A. Silverman, Prentice-Hall, Inc., Englewood Cliffs, N.J., 1962.
11. Peterson, W. W., T. G. Birdsall, and W. C. Fox: The Theory of Signal Detectability, *IRE, Trans. Inform. Theory*, **PGIT-4**: 171 (1954).

Chapter 3

The Extraction of Signals from Noise

The second major topic in communication theory to which we shall apply the statistical methods outlined in Chap. 1 is the extraction of signals from noise. By extraction we mean the separation from, or the measurement of, signal waveform S or some desired parameters of the signal, such as amplitude, frequency, or epoch, in a noise background. Again, we are concerned mainly with optimum systems, and specifically we wish to determine $\boldsymbol{T}_R^{(N)} = (\boldsymbol{T}_R^{(N)})_{\text{ext-opt}}$ in such cases. As in detection (Chap. 2), $(\boldsymbol{T}_R^{(N)})_{\text{ext-opt}}$ embodies the optimum receiver structure for signal extraction. The common criterion of system performance is again taken to be the average risk, and for optimum systems, the corresponding minimum average risk [cf. Eqs. (1.9) and (1.19)]. Performance here, however, is explicitly measured in terms of (actual and) expected error, instead of the error probabilities characteristic of detection problems. The treatment following is a brief account of the elements of signal extraction from this viewpoint, illustrated with a few simple examples of practical interest, where explicit results may be readily obtained.[1,5]

3.1 *Formulation: Average Error, Point, and Interval Estimation*

Let us begin by considering simple estimation, where the time t_λ at which an estimated value is desired occurs at a sampling instant in the available data period $(0,T)$ (cf. Fig. 1.3). As we have already observed from Sec. 1.2, Eq. (1.11), the decision rules in such cases are nonrandomized† and take the form

$$\delta(\gamma|\mathbf{V}) = \delta(\gamma - \gamma_\sigma(\mathbf{V})) \tag{3.1}$$

where the right-hand member is a delta function. Thus,

$$\gamma_\sigma(V) = \boldsymbol{T}_R^{(N)}(\mathbf{V})$$

is the functional operation performed by the receiving system $\boldsymbol{T}_R^{(N)}$ on the received data $\mathbf{V}$ and as such embodies the structure of the estimator. For particular $\mathbf{V} = \mathbf{V}'$, $\gamma_\sigma(\mathbf{V}')$ is an *estimate;* for the process $\mathbf{V}$, $\gamma_\sigma(\mathbf{V})$ is the *estimator*, based on the a priori signal information contained statistically in $\sigma(\mathbf{S})$, or $\sigma(\boldsymbol{\theta})$, where $\boldsymbol{\theta} = (\theta_1, \ldots, \theta_M)$ is a set of M different signal parameters. More explicitly, we often write

$$\gamma = \gamma_\sigma(\boldsymbol{\theta}|\mathbf{V})$$

to indicate that γ is the estimator of $\boldsymbol{\theta}$, given the received data $\mathbf{V}$ and the a priori signal statistics σ. The left member of Eq. (3.1) is a probability density for the usual case of continuous value of $\mathbf{V}$ and for either the $\mathbf{S}$ or $\boldsymbol{\theta}$ under estimation.

When γ_σ is given, i.e., when the receiver is specified, the average risk or error may be determined from Eq. (1.12), which for simple estimation becomes directly

$$R(\sigma,\delta)_S = \int_\Omega \sigma(\mathbf{S})\,\mathbf{dS} \int_\Gamma F_n(\mathbf{V}|\mathbf{S})C(\mathbf{S},\gamma_\sigma)\,\mathbf{dV} \tag{3.2a}$$

or frequently in the deterministic cases, for which $\mathbf{S} = \mathbf{S}(\boldsymbol{\theta})$

$$R(\sigma,\delta)_\theta = \int_{\Omega_\theta} \sigma(\boldsymbol{\theta})\,\mathbf{d\boldsymbol{\theta}} \int_\Gamma W_n(\mathbf{V}|\boldsymbol{\theta})C(\boldsymbol{\theta},\gamma_\sigma)\,\mathbf{dV} \tag{3.2b}$$

where $W_n(\mathbf{V}|\boldsymbol{\theta}) = F_n(\mathbf{V}|\mathbf{S}(\boldsymbol{\theta}))$, usually. Of course, the average risk

† This is true of certain types of cost function C, i.e., convex cost functions; cf. Ref. 1, p. 961.

depends on our choice of the cost, or error, function† C. We may now expect a wider range of possibilities than in detection [where only constant or logarithmic costs—cf. Eqs. (1.7) to (1.10)—have so far proved useful], since for estimation the number of reasonable and acceptable cost functions is now much expanded.

Another type of estimation procedure that is particularly useful in applications is *interval estimation*. This is defined as the probability that a particular estimate γ_σ (for a given $\mathbf{V}$) falls within $(1 \pm \lambda)$ 100 per cent of the true value of the quantity $\mathbf{S}$ (or $\boldsymbol{\theta}$) being estimated, viz.,

$$P[(1-\lambda)\mathbf{S} \leq \gamma_\sigma(\mathbf{S}|\mathbf{V}) \leq (1+\lambda)\mathbf{S}]$$

or $\qquad 0 < \lambda < 1 \qquad (3.3a)$

$$P[(1-\lambda)\boldsymbol{\theta} \leq \gamma_\sigma(\boldsymbol{\theta}|\mathbf{V}) \leq (1+\lambda)(\boldsymbol{\theta})]$$

where in the n-dimensional cases, $\mathbf{S} = (S_1, \ldots, S_n)$, or M-dimensional situations, $\boldsymbol{\theta} = (\theta_1, \ldots, \theta_M)$, respectively.‡ Thus, if $W_n(\gamma_\sigma|\mathbf{S})$ or $W_M(\gamma_\sigma|\boldsymbol{\theta})$ are the d.d.'s of γ_σ for $\mathbf{S}$ or $\boldsymbol{\theta}$, then the probability P, in (3.3a), becomes

$$P[(1-\lambda)\mathbf{S} \leq \gamma_\sigma(\mathbf{S}|\mathbf{V}) \leq (1+\lambda)\mathbf{S}] = \int_{(1-\lambda)S_1}^{(1+\lambda)S_1} \cdots \int_{(1-\lambda)S_n}^{(1+\lambda)S_n} W_n(\gamma_\sigma|\mathbf{S})\, \mathbf{d}\gamma_\sigma \qquad (3.3b)$$

and similarly for $\gamma_\sigma(\boldsymbol{\theta}|\mathbf{V})$. In the case of a single signal parameter θ ($M = 1$), this reduces to the more familiar form

$$P[(1-\lambda)\theta \leq \gamma_\sigma(\theta|\mathbf{V}) \leq (1+\lambda)\theta] = \int_{(1-\lambda)\theta}^{(1+\lambda)\theta} W_1(\gamma_\sigma|\theta)\, d\gamma_\sigma \qquad (3.4)$$

The conditional probability densities

$$p(\gamma|\mathbf{S}) = W_n(\gamma_\sigma|\mathbf{S}), \qquad p(\gamma|\boldsymbol{\theta}) = W_M(\gamma_\sigma|\boldsymbol{\theta})$$

are found from Eq. (1.13) and its obvious modification when $\mathbf{S}$ is replaced by $\boldsymbol{\theta}$. The d.d.'s of the estimators themselves may be obtained from Eq. (1.15) or (1.17).

In statistical parlance, the estimate γ_σ is a *point estimate* and embodies the specific structure of the receiver $\mathbf{T}_R^{(N)}$. On the other hand, *interval*

† It is natural to consider the cost or risk proportional to the error, so that $C(\mathbf{S},\gamma_\sigma)$, etc., may be regarded here equally well as a measure of error (see Sec. 3.2).
‡ More generally, we can assign a different value of λ to each component of $\mathbf{S}$ or $\boldsymbol{\theta}$.

estimation P yields a probability which is a measure of the efficiency of the point estimator in any particular application (each $\mathbf{V}$), while the *average risk R* measures the expected cost or average error in the use of the point estimator, considered over the set of all possible received data $\mathbf{V}$.

Finally, we observe once more that *prediction and smoothing* (e.g., filtering), as well as the simple estimation ($t_\lambda = t_k$) discussed above, can be included at once in the decision-theory formalism. The average risks (or errors) [Eqs. (3.2*a*) and (3.2*b*)] in this instance are given by Eq. (1.12), with the point estimator $\gamma_\sigma = \gamma_\sigma(\mathbf{S}'|\mathbf{V})$ in which $\mathbf{S}'$ is an $(n+1)$-component vector $[\mathbf{S}, f(S_\lambda)]$. The $f(S_\lambda)$ is the predicted, or smoothed, value of S at t_λ, within or without the data interval $(0,T)$ [cf. remarks following Eq. (1.12)].†

3.2 *Optimum Estimation*[4]

As in detection (cf. Chap. 2), we may expect a variety of optima, depending on the choice of cost function and on possible constraints. For the unconstrained case, with deterministic signals, for example, we seek optimal estimators from the solution of‡

$$\delta R_\theta = \int_{\Omega_\theta} \sigma(\boldsymbol{\theta}) W_n(\mathbf{V}|\boldsymbol{\theta}) \left. \frac{\partial C(\boldsymbol{\theta},\boldsymbol{\gamma}_\sigma)}{\partial \boldsymbol{\gamma}} \right|_{\boldsymbol{\gamma}=\boldsymbol{\gamma}^*} d\boldsymbol{\theta} = 0 \tag{3.5}$$

whenever C possesses the required derivatives. The estimator $\boldsymbol{\gamma}^*$ that is the solution of Eq. (3.5) can usually be shown to be the desired optimum, either by inspection or by a direct demonstration that $\delta^2 R_\theta \big|_{\boldsymbol{\gamma}^*} > 0$ for minimum average risk (or error).

Among the most useful and common examples of optimum estimators is that derived from Eq. (3.5) with a *quadratic cost function* (QCF)

$$C(\boldsymbol{\theta},\boldsymbol{\gamma}) = C_0|\boldsymbol{\theta} - \boldsymbol{\gamma}_\sigma|^2 = C_0 \sum_{i=1}^{M} (\theta_i - \gamma_{\sigma i})^2 \tag{3.6}$$

From this it is easily shown that the Bayes error is

$$R_\theta^* = C_0 \min_{\gamma_\sigma} \overline{|\boldsymbol{\theta} - \boldsymbol{\gamma}_\sigma|^2}^{\theta,N} = C_0 \overline{|\boldsymbol{\theta} - \boldsymbol{\gamma}_\sigma^*(\boldsymbol{\theta}|\mathbf{V})|^2}^{V} \tag{3.7}$$

where the optimum estimator is specifically determined from the set of

† Ref. 1, sec. 16.2, and in particular secs. 16.2-2 and 16.3. For a discussion of the Wiener-Kolmogoroff theory of linear prediction and filtering, see Refs. 2 and 3.
‡ Ref. 1, eq. (21.61).

equations†

$$\gamma_\sigma^*(\boldsymbol{\theta}|\mathbf{V}) = \int_{\Omega_\theta} \boldsymbol{\theta}\sigma(\boldsymbol{\theta})W_n(\mathbf{V}|\boldsymbol{\theta})\, \mathbf{d\theta} \Big/ \int_{\Omega_\theta} \sigma(\boldsymbol{\theta})W_n(\mathbf{V}|\boldsymbol{\theta})\, \mathbf{d\theta} \tag{3.8a}$$

or

$$\gamma_\sigma^*(\boldsymbol{\theta}|\mathbf{V}) = \int_{\Omega_\theta} \boldsymbol{\theta} w_n(\mathbf{V},\boldsymbol{\theta})\, \mathbf{d\theta} \Big/ \int_{\Omega_\theta} w_n(\mathbf{V},\boldsymbol{\theta})\, \mathbf{d\theta} \tag{3.8b}$$

in which $w_n(\mathbf{V},\boldsymbol{\theta})$ is the joint d.d. of $\mathbf{V}$ and $\boldsymbol{\theta}$. Observe that in general the Bayes estimator γ^* here is a *nonlinear* operator on the received data $\mathbf{V}$: the optimum receiver $(\boldsymbol{T}_R^{(N)})_{\text{ext-opt}}$ for estimating $\boldsymbol{\theta}$ is a nonlinear system. In fact, for the QCF, γ^* is the conditional expectation of $\boldsymbol{\theta}$, given $\mathbf{V}$.

As an example where a direct variational calculation of γ^* is not possible [i.e., where Eq. (3.5) cannot be used directly, since $\partial C/\partial\gamma$ does not exist] but nevertheless optimum systems may exist and may be obtained, we have the important case of the *simple cost function* (SCF) for extraction:

$$C(\boldsymbol{\theta},\gamma_\sigma) = \sum_{k=1}^{M} [C_E A_k' - (C_E - C_C)\,\delta(\gamma_k - \theta_k)] \tag{3.9}$$

Here the A_k' are positive constants, chosen so that the resulting average risk, or error, is positive or zero for each index k, C_E is the cost associated with an error, and C_c is the cost of a correct estimate, the same for each component θ_k of $\boldsymbol{\theta}_m$. In more compact form Eq. (3.9) can be written

$$C(\boldsymbol{\theta},\gamma_\sigma) = C_0 \sum_{k=1}^{M} [A_k - \delta(\gamma_k - \theta_k)] \tag{3.9a}$$

with appropriate definitions of C_0 and A_k. Accordingly, in this simple cost assignment, errors of all sizes exact the same cost C_E, while all correct decisions (i.e., estimates) cost $C_C < C_E$. The average risk (or error) here is found to be‡

$$R(\sigma,\delta)_\theta = C_0 \sum_{k=1}^{M} \left[A_k - \int_\Gamma \mathfrak{D}_k(\mathbf{V};\sigma,\delta)\, \mathbf{dV}\right] \tag{3.10}$$

where

$$\mathfrak{D}_R(\mathbf{V};\sigma,\delta) = \int_\Delta \sigma(\gamma_k) W_n(\mathbf{V}|\gamma_k)\, \delta(\gamma_k|\mathbf{V})\, d\gamma_k \tag{3.11}$$

and the decision rule δ is now a probability density.

† Ref. 1, sec. 21.2-2 and eq. (21.62).
‡ Ref. 1, sec. 21.2-1.

Minimization of the average risk leads at once to the conditions

$$\delta(\gamma_k|\mathbf{V}) = \delta(\gamma_k - \gamma_k^*(\boldsymbol{\theta}|\mathbf{V})) \qquad \gamma_k = \theta_k \qquad k = 1, \ldots, M \tag{3.12}$$

where the components γ_k^* ($k = 1, \ldots, M$) of the Bayes estimator $\boldsymbol{\gamma}^*$ are determined from the relations

$$\sigma(\gamma_k^*)W_n(\mathbf{V}|\gamma_k^*) \geq \sigma(\theta_k)W_n(\mathbf{V}|\theta_k) \tag{3.13}$$

for each k and for all θ_R in Ω_{θ_K}. *But this is precisely the condition that determines the unconditional maximum likelihood estimators (UMLE's) of* θ_k, *that is*, γ_k^*. Thus, equivalently, the γ_k^* are determined by

$$\frac{\partial}{\partial\theta_k} \log [\sigma(\theta_k)W_n(\mathbf{V}|\theta_k)] \bigg|_{\theta_k = \theta_k^* = \gamma_k^*} = 0 \tag{3.14}$$

where the $\theta_k^* = \gamma_k^*$ are those roots of Eq. (3.14) which *maximize* $\sigma(\theta_k)W_n(\mathbf{V}|\theta_k)$. Note that when the θ_k are *uniformly distributed* in Ω_{θ_k}, Eq. (3.14) reduces to

$$\frac{\partial}{\partial\theta_k} \log W_n(\mathbf{V}|\theta_k) \bigg|_{\theta_k = \theta_k^*} = 0 \tag{3.14a}$$

which is also equivalent to the relation determining *conditional maximum likelihood estimators*† (CMLE's) of θ_k.

From Eq. (3.1) in Eq. (1.13), with $\boldsymbol{\gamma} = \mathbf{S}$ (or $\boldsymbol{\gamma} = \boldsymbol{\theta}$ for parameter estimation), we observe, also, that *the maximum (conditional) likelihood estimator maximizes the probability of a correct decision*, without regard to incorrect decisions and their costs. A similar argument applied to Eq. (3.1) in Eq. (1.15) (with suitable modification when $\boldsymbol{\gamma} = \boldsymbol{\theta}$) shows that the maximum *unconditional* likelihood estimator S^* (or θ^*) maximizes the *average* probability of a correct decision, where all possible signals are taken into account, once more without specific regard for incorrect decisions and their costs.‡

Although the QCF and the SCF are analytically and historically the most familiar, many other cost functions can be constructed which may be more appropriate in special applications.§ Even when such cost functions take the usual difference form $F(\boldsymbol{\theta} - \boldsymbol{\gamma}_\sigma)$, however, explicit optimization is not easily achieved for general statistics of $\mathbf{V}$ and $\boldsymbol{\theta}$, and

† Ref. 1, secs. 21.1 and, in particular, 21.1-2.
‡ Ref. 1, sec. 21.5. See also sec. 23.3-3 for a summary of useful properties of maximum likelihood estimators.
§ Ref. 1, sec. 21.2-3.

little is known as yet in a systematic way about the (point and interval) Bayes estimators in these cases. But under certain rather broad conditions we can escape from the occasionally too restrictive and inappropriate natures of the QCF and SCF with the help of the following two theorems.†

Theorem 1. If the joint d.d. $w_n(\mathbf{V},\boldsymbol{\theta})$ can be factored into the form $w_n(\mathbf{V},\boldsymbol{\theta}) = f_1(\mathbf{V}) f_2(\boldsymbol{\theta} - \mathbf{g}(\mathbf{V}))$, where f_1 and g are any functions of $\mathbf{V}$, and if $f_2(\boldsymbol{\theta} - \mathbf{g}(\mathbf{V})) = f_2(g(\mathbf{V}) - \boldsymbol{\theta})$, i.e., f_2 is symmetrical and also is unimodal about $\boldsymbol{\theta} = \mathbf{g}(\mathbf{V})$, where the ranges of $\boldsymbol{\theta}$ are $(-\infty, \infty)$, then for differentiable‡ cost criteria [Eq. (3.5)], the Bayes estimator is

$$\boldsymbol{\gamma}_\sigma^*(\mathbf{V}) = \mathbf{g}(\mathbf{V}) \tag{3.15a}$$

Theorem 2. Let cost functions of the type $C(\theta - \gamma_\sigma)$ have the properties that

$$\begin{aligned} C(\theta - \gamma_\sigma) &= C(\gamma_\sigma - \theta) \\ C([\theta - \gamma_\sigma]_1) < C([\theta - \gamma_\sigma]_2) &\qquad \text{if } |[\theta - \gamma_\sigma]_1| < |[\theta - \gamma_\sigma]_2| \end{aligned} \tag{3.15b}$$

Then the Bayes estimator γ_{QCF}^* for the QCF $(\theta - \gamma_\sigma)^2$ also minimizes the average risk for these other cost functions [Eqs. (3.15*b*)], provided the conditional d.d. of θ given $\mathbf{V}$, i.e., $w(\theta|\mathbf{V})$, is unimodal and symmetrical about this mode $(\theta = \gamma_\sigma^*)$.

Typical cost functions obeying Eqs. (3.15*b*) and satisfying the other conditions of theorem 2, so that γ_{QCF}^* is consequently the optimum estimator, are

$$C_1(\theta - \gamma_\sigma^*) = |\theta - \gamma_\sigma^*| \tag{3.16a}$$

$$\begin{aligned} C_2(\theta - \gamma_\sigma^*) &= 0 \qquad |\theta - \gamma_\sigma^*| < A \qquad \gamma_\sigma^* = \gamma_{\mathrm{QCF}}^* \\ &= 1 \qquad |\theta - \gamma_\sigma^*| > A \end{aligned} \tag{3.16b}$$

Figure 3.1 shows cost functions of the type discussed here and previously in this section.

Theorem 2 may be extended in straightforward fashion to the multiparameter cases $\boldsymbol{\theta} = (\theta_1, \ldots, \theta_M)$. Similarly, when it is a question of waveform extraction, $C(\boldsymbol{\theta},\gamma_\sigma)$ is replaced by $C(\mathbf{S},\gamma_\sigma)$, etc., in Eqs. (3.5) to (3.16). Interval estimation, prediction, and filtering, with these and similar cost functions, may be handled in the same way. The basic

† Ref. 1, sec. 21.2-3.
‡ See footnote, p. 973, Ref. 1.

expression for average risk or error is still Eq. (1.12), which again, in general, yields *nonlinear* operators. Still other cost functions may have desirable properties in applications. In certain cases when $w(\boldsymbol{\theta})$, or $\sigma(\mathbf{S})$, is uniform, then γ^*_{QCF} may have Minimax properties† [cf. Eq.

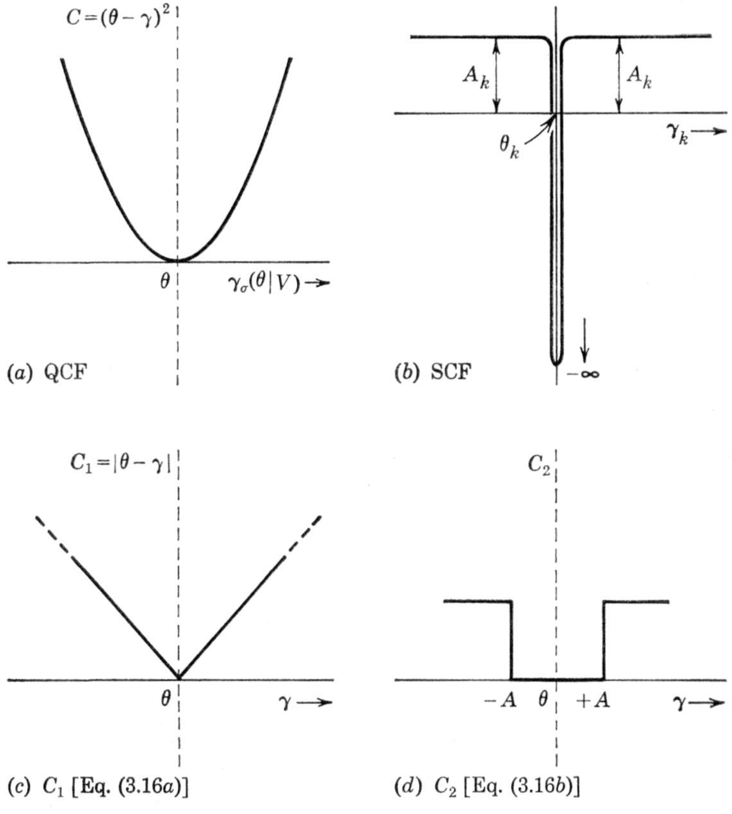

Fig. 3.1 Some typical cost functions in the theory of signal extraction.

(1.22) et seq.]. If $w_n(\mathbf{V},\boldsymbol{\theta})$ possesses certain symmetry properties, then the Bayes estimator may often be found directly from the symmetry structure.‡ Not only Bayes extraction, but also optimum extraction based on minimizing the average equivocation [cf. Eq. (1.10)], as in

† Ref. 1, sec. 21.2-2, pp. 968–970; sec. 22.3-2.
‡ Ref. 1, sec. 21.2-3 (theorem I); sec. 21.5, p. 1005; and sec. 22.3-2, p. 1022.

detection, are possible.† Also as in detection, we may turn to more sophisticated extraction procedures, for example, sequential estimation and adaptive systems that use dynamic-programming techniques.[5]

One important application of the present theory is the estimation of signal amplitudes when the signals are observed in the presence of noise. Amplitude estimation is of interest in a variety of situations: to set detection thresholds in common feedback links; to determine signal-to-noise ratios and adjust decision thresholds for automatic gain control; in radar, to measure target cross sections and, generally, whenever desired information appears as amplitude variations of a waveform or requires the measurement of signal energy, classification, and the identification of signals. The following sections are devoted principally to examples of amplitude estimation when the signals are deterministic. The case of waveform estimation for random signals is considered elsewhere.‡

3.3 *A Simple Example: Coherent Estimation of Signal Amplitude*§

We may illustrate the preceding generalities with a simple but important example, where a fairly complete theory is easily constructed. This occurs for the coherent estimation of the amplitude $\theta = (a_0)$ of deterministic signals in noise backgrounds when the noise is gaussian and when the a priori d.d. $\sigma(a_0)$ also has a normal distribution

$$\sigma(\boldsymbol{\theta}) = \sigma(a_0) = (2\pi\sigma^2)^{-1/2} e^{-(a_0-\bar{a}_0)^2/2\sigma^2} \qquad \sigma^2 = \overline{a_0^2} - \bar{a}_0^2 \quad (3.17)$$

Again we assume that the signal and noise are additive and normalized [cf. Eqs. (2.40) to (2.42)], so that

$$\mathbf{S} = a_0\sqrt{\psi}\,\mathbf{s} \qquad \mathbf{V} = \mathbf{S} + \mathbf{N} = \sqrt{\psi}\,\mathbf{v} \qquad \psi = \overline{\mathbf{N}^2};\ \bar{\mathbf{N}} = 0 \quad (3.18)$$

Let us determine first the Bayes (point) estimator with QCF. This is found from Eqs. (3.8), where $w_n(\mathbf{V},\theta) = w_n(\mathbf{V},a_0)$ is simply the product of Eqs. (2.41) and (3.17). The Bayes estimator $\gamma_\sigma^* = a_0^*$ here is specifically for discrete sampling on $(0,T)$

$$T_R^{(N)}(\mathbf{V})_{\text{opt-ext}} = a_0^*(\mathbf{V})_{\text{QCF}} = \frac{\Phi_v + \bar{a}_0/\sigma^2}{\Phi_s + 1/\sigma^2} \equiv a\Phi_v + b \quad (3.19)$$

† Ref. 1, sec. 22.3-2.
‡ Ref. 1, sec. 21.1-3(2) for maximum likelihood estimation of waveform (SCF) and secs. 21.4-1 and 21.4-2 for waveform estimation with QCF.
§ See also Ref. 1, sec. 21.3-1.

where again $\Phi_v = \tilde{\mathbf{s}}\mathbf{k}_N^{-1}\mathbf{v}$, $\Phi_s = \tilde{\mathbf{s}}\mathbf{k}_N^{-1}\mathbf{s}$ [cf. Eq. (2.43) et seq. and the Appendix] and a, b are defined by the last relation in Eq. (3.19). Because of the assumed normal statistics and complete knowledge of the signal at the receiver (except for amplitude), this optimum estimator is linear in **V**. With continuous sampling on $(0,T)$ we replace Φ_v, Φ_s by $(\Phi_T)_v$, $(\Phi_T)_s$ respectively; cf. Eqs. (2.51). As in the simple detection problem of Sec. 2.5, the optimum receiver here requires the cross correlation of the received wave $V(t)$ with the known, locally generated signal *waveform* $s(t - \epsilon_0,\theta_0)$, weighted according to Eq. (3.19). When the background noise is white, we have for the (unnormalized) amplitude estimator

$$A_0^*(V)\Big|_{\text{white-QCF}} = \lim_{\psi\to\infty} \sqrt{2\psi}\, a_0^*\Big|_{\text{QCF}}$$
$$= \frac{\sqrt{2}\left[(1/W_0)\int_0^T V(t)s(t-\epsilon_0;\,\boldsymbol{\theta}_0)\,dt + \overline{A_0}/\sqrt{2}\,\sigma_A^2\right]}{(1/W_0)\int_0^T s(t-\epsilon_0;\,\boldsymbol{\theta}_0)^2\,dt + \sigma_A^{-2}} \tag{3.20}$$

where $\sigma_A^2 = \overline{A_0^2} - \overline{A_0}^2$, etc. [since $\sigma_A^2 \equiv 2\psi\sigma^2$; cf. Eq. (3.17)]. Note also that in the limiting situation where $\sigma_A \to \infty$ (a uniform d.d. of amplitudes, for example), A_0^* here is independent of the spectral intensity of the noise.

The Bayes estimator a_{QCF}^*, Eq. (3.19) above, is also normally distributed, since Φ_v is linear in **V** and since the noise *and* the signal amplitudes a_0 are themselves normally distributed. We find specifically that†

$$w_1(a_0^*)_{\text{QCF}} = \frac{e^{-(a_0^*-\overline{a_0})^2/2[\sigma^4\Phi_s/(1+\sigma^2\Phi_s)]}}{[2\pi\sigma^4\Phi_s/(1+\sigma^2\Phi_s)]^{1/2}} \tag{3.21a}$$

with the c.f.

$$F_1^*(i\xi)_{a_0^*} = e^{i\xi\overline{a_0} - \frac{\sigma^4\Phi_s}{2}\xi^2/(1+\sigma^2\Phi_s)} \tag{3.21b}$$

The first and second (unconditional) moments of a_0^* are

$$\overline{a_0^*} = \overline{a_0} \qquad \overline{a_0^{*2}} = \overline{a_0}^2 + \frac{\sigma^4\Phi_s}{1+\sigma^2\Phi_s} \tag{3.21c}$$

The estimator a_0^* is accordingly *unbiased*. Similarly, the d.d. of $a_0^* - a_0$ is also normal, such that‡

$$w_1(a_0^* - a_0)_{\text{QCF}} = \frac{e^{-(a_0^*-a_0)^2/[2\sigma^2/(\sigma^2\Phi_s+1)]}}{[2\pi\sigma^2/(\sigma^2\Phi_s+1)]^{1/2}} \tag{3.22a}$$

† Ref. 1, pp. 981 and 982.
‡ Ref. 1, pp. 981 and 982.

with

$$F_1^*(i\xi)_{a_0^*-a_0} = e^{-\sigma^2\xi^2/2(\sigma^2\Phi_s+1)} \tag{3.22b}$$

and

$$\overline{(a_0^* - a_0)}^{N,a_0} = 0 \qquad \overline{(a_0^* - a_0)^2}^{N,a_0} = \frac{\sigma^2}{\sigma^2\Phi_s + 1} \tag{3.22c}$$

Accordingly, the Bayes risk, or error, here is at once from Eq. (3.22*c*) in Eq. (3.7)

$$R^*(\sigma,\delta)_{a_0} = C_0(\overline{a_0^{*2}} - \overline{2a_0a_0^*} + \overline{a_0^2}) = \frac{C_0\sigma^2}{\sigma^2\Phi_s + 1} \tag{3.23}$$

As expected when $\sigma^2 \to 0$, the average error vanishes, since extraction is exact on the average ($a_0^* = \bar{a}_0 = a_0$), while when $\sigma^2 \to \infty$ there is necessarily always a finite average error $C_0\Phi_s^{-1}$. The Bayes error, of course, depends on the waveform of the signal and on the covariance function of the accompanying noise. (The present example is of interest when signals subject to fading are received in noise; here $\bar{a}_0$ is usually large and σ may be small, so that a_0 is essentially always greater than zero.) We can show also that as $\sigma^2 \to \infty$, $a_{QCF}^* = \Phi_v/\Phi_s$ is a Minimax estimate [cf. Eq. (3.29)], with Minimax average error $R_M^* = C_0\Phi_s^{-1}$ ($>R^*$). With white noise backgrounds the Bayes risk, or error, Eq. (3.23), becomes

$$\hat{R}^*\Big|_{\text{white}} = \lim_{\psi\to\infty} 2\psi R_{a_0}^* = C_0\sigma_A^2(1 + 2\sigma_A^2\bar{E}_s/\overline{A_0^2}W_0)^{-1} \tag{3.24}$$

where again $\bar{E}_s$ is the average received signal energy; cf. (2.53). The Minimax average error here is ($\sigma_A^2 \to \infty$)

$$\hat{R}_M^*\Big|_{\text{white}} = C_0\overline{A_0^2}W_0/2\bar{E}_s \tag{3.25}$$

To provide the interval estimation of a_0 according to Eq. (3.4) we need the conditional d.d. $w_1(a_0^*|a_0)$. This may be found by determining the characteristic function $F_{a_0^*}(i\xi|a_0) = \mathbf{E}_{N|a_0}\{e^{i\xi a_0^*}\} = \langle e^{i\xi a_0^*}\rangle_{N|a_0}$ and the desired d.d. $w_1(a_0^*|a_0)$ by inversion in the usual way. More simply, since a_0^* is linear in $\mathbf{V}$, and hence in $\mathbf{N}$, which by Eq. (3.18) is normally distributed, $w_1(a_0^*|a_0)$ is also normal, with the conditional average and conditional variance

$$\overline{a_0^*}^{N|a_0} = \frac{a_0\Phi_s + \bar{a}_0/\sigma^2}{\Phi_s + 1/\sigma^2} \qquad \sigma^2_{a_0^*|a_0} = \frac{\sigma^4\Phi_s}{(\Phi_s\sigma^2 + 1)^2} \tag{3.26}$$

Accordingly, the probability P that the optimum estimator a_{QCF}^* [Eq.

(3.19)] lies within $\pm 100\lambda$ per cent of the true value a_0 becomes specifically

$$P[(1-\lambda)a_0 \leq a_0^* \leq (1+\lambda)a_0] = \tfrac{1}{2}\Theta\left[\sigma_0\left(\frac{a_0 - \bar{a}_0 + \lambda(1+\sigma^2\Phi_s)}{\sigma^2\Phi_s}\right)\right] - \tfrac{1}{2}\Theta\left[\sigma_0\left(\frac{a_0 - \bar{a}_0 - \lambda(1+\sigma^2\Phi_s)}{\sigma^2\Phi_s}\right)\right] \quad (3.27)$$

where σ_0^2 [Eq. (2.48)] is the (actual) output signal-to-noise ratio; $\Phi_s/2$ is the processing gain. With large processing gains, so that σ_0^2 is large, Eq. (3.27) approaches unity, as expected, as is also the case when

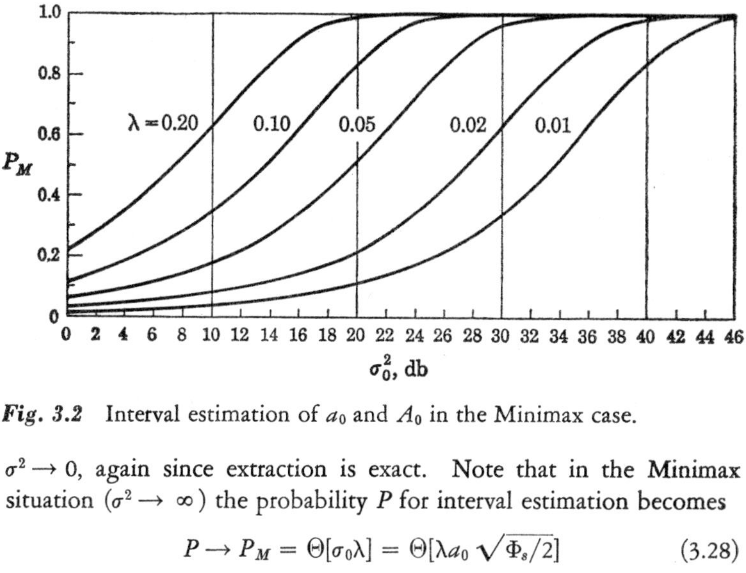

Fig. 3.2 Interval estimation of a_0 and A_0 in the Minimax case.

$\sigma^2 \to 0$, again since extraction is exact. Note that in the Minimax situation ($\sigma^2 \to \infty$) the probability P for interval estimation becomes

$$P \to P_M = \Theta[\sigma_0\lambda] = \Theta[\lambda a_0 \sqrt{\Phi_s/2}] \quad (3.28)$$

which is shown in Fig. 3.2 as a function of output signal-to-noise ratio σ_0^2 (db) $= 10 \log_{10} \sigma_0^2$. The conditional risk r^*_{QCF} is also found at once from Eq. (3.26), for by definition

$$r^*_{\text{QCF}} = C_0\sigma^2_{a_0^*|a_0} = \frac{C_0\sigma^4\Phi_s}{(\sigma^2\Phi_s + 1)^2} \quad (3.29)$$

and when $\sigma^2 \to \infty$, we see that $r^*_{\text{QCF}} \simeq C_0/\Phi_s$, independent of a_0, thus establishing the Minimax character of $a^*_{0-\text{QCF}}$ in this limiting situation.†

† Ref. 1, p. 798, theorem 7.

When the background noise is white (and when continuous sampling is used), we find that the conditional average and variance of a_0^* [Eq. (3.26)] become

$$\overline{A_0^*}^{N|a_0} = \frac{(2E_s\sigma_A^2/A_0W_0 + \overline{A_0})}{1 + 2\sigma_A^2E_s/A_0^2W_0} \qquad \sigma^2_{A_0^*|A_0} = \frac{2E_s\sigma_A^2/A_0^2W_0}{(1 + 2\sigma_A^2E_s/A_0^2W_0)^2} \tag{3.30}$$

with corresponding modifications in P and $r^*_{QCF}\Big|_{white} = \lim_{\psi\to\infty} 2\psi r^*_{QCF}$, where $\sigma_0^2\Big|_{white} = E_s/W_0$, $A_0 = \sqrt{2\psi}\, a_0$, etc. [cf. (2.53)].

The Bayes estimator of amplitude, Eq. (3.19), is also optimum for a wide class of cost functions other than the QCF assumed above. For we observe at once from Eqs. (3.22) that the conditional d.d. of $z \equiv a_0^* - a_0$, given $\mathbf{V}$ [i.e., $a_0^* = a_0^*(\mathbf{V})$] is the same as the conditional d.d. $w(a_0|\mathbf{V})$ and, furthermore, $w(a_0|\mathbf{V})$ is unimodal and symmetrical about the mode (here, a_0^*). The conditions of the theorem [Eq. (3.15) et seq.] are accordingly met, so that a^*_{QCF}, Eq. (3.19), also minimizes the average risk or error for cost functions of the type described in Eq. (3.16).

Let us turn now to the error criterion based on the simple cost function [cf. Eq. (3.9) et seq.], which as we have shown above [Eqs. (3.13 and (3.14)] is for minimum average error equivalent to (unconditional) maximum likelihood estimation. With Eqs. (2.41) and (3.17) in Eq. (3.14) and $\theta_k = a_0$, we find that *the determining relation for* a^*_{SCF} *is simply Eq. (3.19) once more*, i.e., $a^*_{SCF} = a^*_{QCF}$ for the gaussian a priori d.d. of amplitudes (3.17) postulated here. Moreover, with a *uniform* d.d. of amplitudes, σ^2 becomes infinite; so we have†

$$a^*_{SCF} = a^*_{QCF} = \Phi_v/\Phi_s \tag{3.31}$$

for which

$$w(a_0|V) = w(a_0 - a_0^*|V) = \sqrt{\frac{\Phi_s}{2\pi}}\, e^{-\frac{1}{2}\Phi_s(a_0-\Phi_v/\Phi_s)^2} \tag{3.32}$$

[cf. Eq. (3.22*a*) with $\sigma^2 \to \infty$]. Similarly, Eqs. (3.21*a*) to (3.21*c*) also apply for a^*_{SCF}, as does Eq. (3.20) for white noise backgrounds. Finally, we observe that with the uniform d.d. of amplitudes ($\sigma^2 \to \infty$) the conditional and unconditional maximum likelihood estimators are equal [and Eqs. (3.26) to (3.30) likewise remain unchanged for a^*_{SCF} here].

† Ref. 1, eq. (21.25).

3.4 *Extensions: Incoherent Estimation of Signal Amplitudes*[6] †

A second example of some practical interest, and one for which a well-developed theory is also available, is the estimation of signal amplitude in the case of narrow-band deterministic signals that are now *incoherently* observed in normal noise. Here $\boldsymbol{\theta} = a_0$, $\sigma(\boldsymbol{\theta}) = \sigma(a_0)$ once more (cf. example above). The (normalized) signal waveform is given by Eq. (2.56) and is known at the receiver, and in the usual situation of uniformly distributed carrier phase (or epoch) one then readily establishes that the Bayes estimators for the QCF and the SCF [Eqs. (3.8) and (3.14), respectively] become for continuous sampling on $(0,T)$†

$$\begin{aligned} \boldsymbol{T}_R^{(N)}(V)_{\text{opt-ext}} &= \overset{*}{a}_{\text{QCF}}(V(t)) \\ &= \int a_0\sigma(a_0)e^{-a_0^2B_T/2}I_0(a_0\Psi_0^{1/2})\,da_0 \Big/ \int\sigma(a_0)e^{-a_0^2B_T/2}I_0(a_0\Psi_0^{1/2})\,da_0 \end{aligned} \tag{3.33}$$

and for the SCF, $\overset{*}{a}_{0\text{-SCF}}$ is determined as the root of

$$\left[\frac{\sigma'(a_0)}{\sigma(a_0)} + \Psi_0^{1/2}\frac{I_1(a_0\Psi_0^{1/2})}{I_0(a_0\Psi_0^{1/2})} - a_0B_T\right]_{a_0=a_0^*\text{-SCF}} = 0 \tag{3.34}$$

which absolutely maximizes the joint d.d. $w_n(\mathbf{V},a_0)$ (here in the limit $n \to \infty$ for continuous sampling); B_T and Ψ_0 are given by Eqs. (2.58*a*) and (2.58*b*). The respective Bayes errors [Eqs. (3.7) and (3.10)] are also found to be‡

$$R^*_{\text{QCF}} = C_0\int\sigma(a_0)\,da_0\int_0^\infty[a_0 - a_0^*(x)_{\text{QCF}}]^2W_1(x|a_0)\,dx \tag{3.35}$$

and

$$R^*_{\text{SCF}} = C_0\left[A_1 - \int_0^\infty\sigma(a_0^*(x))W_1(x|a_0^*(x))\,dx\right] \tag{3.36}$$

where $W_1(x|a_0)$ is the conditional d.d. of x $(\equiv\Psi_0^{1/2})$, given a_0 (≥ 0), viz.,§

$$W_1(x|a_0) = xe^{-x^2/2B_T - a_0^2B_T/2}I_0(a_0x)/B_T \qquad x \geq 0 \tag{3.37}$$

In the case of interval estimation we use Eq. (3.4) with $\theta = a_0$, and γ_σ,

† Ref. 1, sec. 21.3-2. This includes the initial formulation by discrete sampling on $(0,T)$; see also Ref. 6, pp. 366–368.
‡ Ref. 6, pp. 368–370.
§ This d.d also may be obtained from Eq. (2.62) and the relation

$$W_1(x|a_0) = w_1(z|H_1)|dz/dx|,$$

since by Eq. (2.59) $z = a_0^2x^2$, $\sigma^2 = a_0^2B_T/2$.

$d\gamma_\sigma$ replaced by a_0^*, da_0^*, where now $W_1(a_0^*|a_0) \neq W_1(x|a_0)$ in general; however, see Eq. (3.59).

We observe that since a_0^* depends here only on the received wave $V(t)$ through the functional $\Psi_0(V)$, the optimum receiver $T_R^{(N)}(V)_{\text{opt-ext}}$ can be resolved into two parts, one that depends only on Ψ_0 and the other, $a_0^* = F(\Psi_0)$, whose structure F is determined by (1) the a priori d.d. of a_0 and (2) the particular choice of cost or error function. Thus, optimum receiver structure here consists of the *same type of nonlinear operation as in the corresponding detection situation*† [cf. Eqs. (2.59) and (2.65)], but instead of comparing $a_0^2\Psi_0$ or other appropriate functions of Ψ_0 against a threshold, we further process the number Ψ_0 in accordance with the particular $F(\Psi_0)$ required for the Bayes estimator. The fact that a_0^* here depends only on $\Psi_0(V)$ is fundamentally attributable to the model in question: narrow-band *deterministic* signals (of known waveform), incoherently observed in *normal* noise, *with a uniform d.d. of RF epochs* and where all other parameters of the signal (and noise) are known at the receiver (except signal amplitude, of course). When any feature of this model is perturbed, more complex structures for a_0^* and more complicated forms for Bayes error may be expected.

From Eqs. (3.33) to (3.36) it is evident that explicit a priori d.d.'s are required if explicit results are to be obtained. Two common and useful d.d.'s are the‡

Rayleigh d.d.:

$$\begin{aligned} \sigma(a_0) &= \frac{a_0 e^{-a_0^2/2P_0}}{P_0} && a_0 \geq 0 \\ \sigma(a_0) &= 0 && a_0 < 0 \\ P_0 &= \overline{a_{0R}^2}/2 \end{aligned} \tag{3.38}$$

and the uniform d.d.:

$$\begin{aligned} \sigma(a_0) &= P_u^{-1/2} && 0 < a_0 < P_u^{1/2} \\ \sigma(a_0) &= 0 && \text{elsewhere} \\ P_u &= 3\overline{a_{0u}^2} \end{aligned} \tag{3.39}$$

The Rayleigh d.d. is often representative of certain types of (slow) fading, while the uniform d.d has certain Minimax properties,§ among others.

† For further details, see Sec. 4.1.
‡ Ref. 6, p. 370; Ref. 1, p. 950.
§ Ref. 1, sec. 21.2-2 and pp. 969 and 970.

With these a priori d.d.'s exact expressions for the Bayes estimators a_0^* [Eqs. (3.33) and (3.34)] can in certain cases be found, as we note below. However, in most practical applications it is sufficient to consider a strong-signal theory, where the effective output signal-to-noise ratio [again defined by Eq. (2.64)] is large, either because the input ratio (a_0) is strong or because the processing gain $B_T/2$ is sufficiently great (so-called *threshold operation*, where $a_0^2 B_T/2 \gg 1$, etc., with $a_0^2 \ll 1$). In fact, in the limit of infinite processing gain or for indefinitely large average input ratios ($\overline{a_{0u}^2}, \overline{a_{0R}^2} \to \infty$) the Bayes estimators a^* approach asymptotically the same limiting form, with the broad canonical properties summarized in Sec. 3.5. Accordingly, let us consider the strong-signal results for a_0^* with QCF and SCF: Eq. (3.38) in Eq. (3.33) yields the exact expression†

$$a_{\mathrm{QCF}}^*\Big|_{\mathrm{Rayleigh}} = \left[\frac{\pi}{2B_T(1+\eta_R)}\right]^{1/2} {}_1F_1\left[-\tfrac{1}{2};1;\frac{-\Psi_0}{2B_T(1+\eta_R)}\right] \qquad \eta_R \equiv (P_0 B_T)^{-1} = 1/\sigma_R^2 \tag{3.40}$$

while with $P_u \to \infty$ (for the strong-signal situations) (3.39) in (3.33) gives‡

$$a_{\mathrm{QCF}}^*\Big|_{\mathrm{uniform}} = \left(\frac{\pi B_T}{2}\right)^{-1/2} {}_1F_1(\tfrac{1}{2};1;-\Psi_0/2B_T)^{-1} \tag{3.41}$$

These relations may be alternatively expressed in the more convenient forms§

Rayleigh:

$$\begin{aligned} a_{\mathrm{QCF}}^* &\simeq x_0\left[\frac{1}{1+\eta_R}+\frac{1}{2B_T x_0^2}+\frac{1+\eta_R}{8B_T^2 x_0^4}+O(B_T^{-3}x_0^{-6})\right.\\ &= x_0\left[1+\frac{1}{B_T}\left(\frac{1}{2x_0^2}-\frac{2}{\overline{a_{0R}^2}}\right)+\frac{1}{B_T^2}\left(\frac{1}{8x_0^4}+\frac{4}{\overline{a_{0R}^2}^{\,2}}\right)+\cdots\right] \end{aligned} \tag{3.42}$$

uniform:

$$a_{\mathrm{QCF}}^* \simeq x_0\left[1+\frac{1}{8B_T x_0}\left(3-\frac{1}{x_0}\right)+\cdots\right] \tag{3.43}$$

† Ref. 1, eqs. (21.109) and (21.112); Ref. 6, eqs. (80*a*) and (80*b*).
‡ *Ibid.*
§ Ref. 6, p. 385.

where $$x_0 \equiv \sqrt{\Psi_0/B_T} \tag{3.44}$$

Figure 3.3 shows a^*_{QCF}, for Eqs. (3.40) and (3.41).

In the case of the SCF, we readily find that the Bayes estimators a^*_{SCF} are now determined from Eqs. (3.38) and (3.39) in Eq. (3.34), which

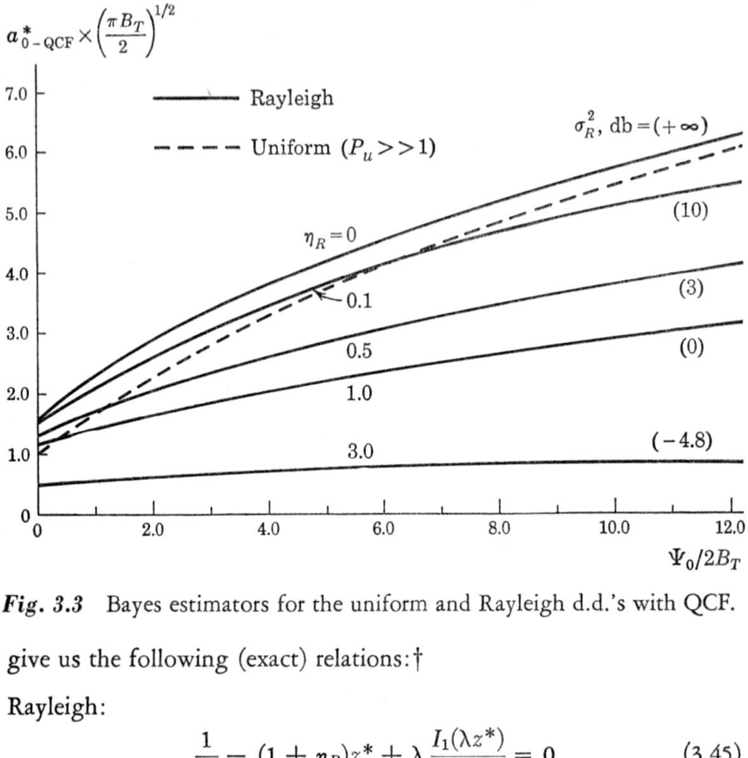

Fig. 3.3 Bayes estimators for the uniform and Rayleigh d.d.'s with QCF.

give us the following (exact) relations:†

Rayleigh:

$$\frac{1}{z^*} - (1 + \eta_R)z^* + \lambda \frac{I_1(\lambda z^*)}{I_0(\lambda z^*)} = 0 \tag{3.45}$$

uniform:

$$\frac{\lambda I_1(\lambda z^*)}{I_0(\lambda z^*)} = z^* \tag{3.46}$$

where

$$\lambda \equiv \sqrt{\Psi_0/B_T} \qquad z^* \equiv a^*_{\text{SCF}}\sqrt{B_T} \tag{3.46a}$$

In the strong-signal situation we easily show with the help of the

† Ref. 6, eqs. (69*a*) and (69*b*) and pp. 386 and 387; Ref. 1, eqs. (21.122*a*) and (122*b*).

asymptotic developments of I_0, I_1 that the a^*_{SCF} now become

Rayleigh:

$$a^*_{\mathrm{SCF}} \simeq x_0 \left[\frac{1}{1+\eta_R} + \frac{1}{2B_T x_0} + O\left(\frac{1+\eta_R}{B_T^4 x_0^4} \right) \right] \tag{3.47}$$

or

$$z^* \simeq \frac{\lambda}{1+\eta_R} + \frac{1}{2\lambda} + O\left(\frac{1+\eta_R}{\lambda^3} \right) \tag{3.47a}$$

uniform:

$$a^*_{\mathrm{SCF}} \simeq x_0 \left[1 - \frac{1}{2B_T x_0} - O\left(\frac{1}{B_T^4 x_0^4} \right) \right] \tag{3.48}$$

or

$$z^* \simeq \lambda - \frac{1}{2\lambda} - O(1/\lambda^3) \tag{3.48a}$$

Figure 3.4 shows a^*_{SCF} for Eqs. (3.45) and (3.46), in both the weak- and strong-signal conditions.

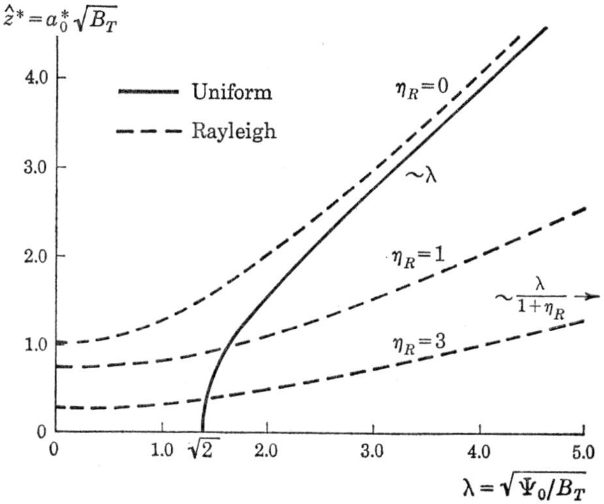

Fig. 3.4 Bayes estimators for the uniform and Rayleigh d.d.'s with SCF.

The important feature to note here is the common asymptotic limit for a^*_{QCF} and a^*_{SCF}, viz.,

$$a_0^* \simeq x_0 = \sqrt{\Psi_0}/B_T \tag{3.49}$$

as the processing gain ($B_T/2$) or the (average) input signal-to-noise ratio [a_{0R}^2, $\overline{a_{0R}^2}$ ($\approx x_0$)], or both, become indefinitely large. In fact, as we shall observe in Sec. 3.5, this is an example of a more general, canonical behavior. Limiting optimum receiver structure consists now specifically of a nonlinear system† determining $\Psi_0(V)$, as in the analogous detection situations (Sec. 2.6), and a simple computer, which obtains $\sqrt{\Psi_0/B_T}$, with B_T, of course, predetermined at the receiver.

The Bayes error is next calculated from Eqs. (3.35) and (3.36), with the appropriate relation for $a_0^*(x)$. Explicit results are generally possible only in the weak- and strong-signal cases,‡ where comparatively simple expressions for $a_0^*(x)$ occur.§ With QCF the Bayes error is found to be

$$R_{\text{QCF}}^* \simeq C_0/B_T + O(B_T^{-2}) \tag{3.50}$$

which to this degree of approximation is *invariant of the a priori distribution.* On the other hand, the Bayes error with SCF becomes‖

$$R_{\text{SCF-Rayleigh}}^* \simeq \frac{C_0}{\sqrt{2\pi\overline{a_{0R}^2}}}\left[\frac{\log \sigma_R^2 + 1.159}{16\sigma_R^2} + O\left(\frac{\log \sigma_R^2}{\sigma_R^3}\right)\right]$$

$$\sigma_R^2 = \frac{1}{\eta_R} \gg 1 \tag{3.51}$$

for the Rayleigh case, and

$$R_{\text{SCF-uniform}}^* \simeq \frac{C_0}{\sqrt{2\pi\overline{a_{0u}^2}}}\left[\frac{1}{24\sqrt{2}\,\sigma_u} + \frac{1}{768\sqrt{2}\,\sigma_u^3} + \cdots\right]$$

$$\sigma_u^2 \gg 1 \tag{3.52}$$

with $\sigma_u^2 \equiv \overline{a_{0u}^2}B_T/2$, in the case of the uniform distribution.¶

When the background noise is white, the Bayes estimators and errors are obtained once more from $A_0^* = \sqrt{2\psi}\; a_0^*$ and $\hat{R}^* = 2\psi R^*$ as $\psi \to \infty$. Thus, for example, the limiting form (3.49) now becomes

$$A_0^*\Big|_{\text{white}} \simeq 2\sqrt{2}\left|\int_0^T V(t)F_s(t)e^{i[\omega_0 t-\varphi_s(t)]}\,dt\right| \Big/ \int_0^T F_s^2(t)\,dt \tag{3.53}$$

[cf. Eq. (2.68)], while Eq. (3.50) reduces to

$$\hat{R}_{\text{QCF}}^* \simeq \frac{2\psi C_0}{B_T} = W_0 C_0 \Big/ \tfrac{1}{2}\int_0^T F_s(t)^2\,dt \tag{3.54}$$

† For details, see Sec. 4.3.

‡ Ref. 6, pp. 383–385 for weak-signal and pp. 386–389, with Appendix 1, for strong-signal cases.

§ Ref. 6, p. 383, and cf. Eq. (3.49).

‖ Ref. 6, figs. 3 and 4.

¶ Ref. 6, figs. 3 and 4.

with the output ratios $\sigma^2_{u,R} = \overline{E_s}^{u,R}/W_0$ [cf. Eqs. (2.70), (2.71), etc.]. Observe in this limiting case that the Bayes estimator (3.53) *is also independent of the spectral density* W_0 *of the background noise*, although the associated mean-square error is proportional to W_0, as in the Minimax cases of the preceding coherent example; cf. Eq. (3.20) as $\sigma_A \to \infty$, and Eq. (3.25).

3.5 *Some Canonical Results*†

When in the examples in Secs. 3.3 and 3.4 the processed signal is sufficiently strong, limiting forms of the optimum amplitude estimators a_0^* can be obtained that are independent of both the a priori distribution $\sigma(a_0)$ of amplitudes and of the choice of error function, for a very broad class of each. This can be shown by first demonstrating for general classes of $\sigma(a_0)$ that a^*_{QCF} is invariant of $\sigma(a_0)$ in the limit of indefinitely large processing gains ($\sim B_T$). Next, one can show that this limiting a^*_{QCF} has the desired statistical properties to permit the application of Theorem 2 [cf. Eq. (3.15*b*)], so that a^*_{QCF} is likewise optimum for other wide classes of error [or cost functions (SCF, etc.)]. Thus, it is in this sense, i.e., with respect to the general classes of $\sigma(a_0)$ and cost functions [of the type (3.15*b*)], that a^*_{QCF} is said to be canonical.

We start with Eq. (2.41) in Eqs. (3.8) for the coherent cases of Sec. 3.3, and with Eq. (3.33) for the incoherent, narrow-band examples of Sec. 3.4. Using the asymptotic development of I_0 for the latter, we see that a^*_{QCF} can be written after completing squares in the various exponentials of the integrands, as

coherent:‡

$$a^*_{\mathrm{QCF}} = \int a_0\sigma(a_0)e^{-\frac{1}{2}\Phi_s(a_0-\Phi_v/\Phi_s)^2}\,da_0 \Big/ \int \sigma(a_0)e^{-\frac{1}{2}\Phi_s(a_0-\Phi_v/\Phi_s)^2}\,da_0 \tag{3.55}$$

and

incoherent:

$$a^*_{\mathrm{QCF}} \simeq \int a_0 g(a_0)e^{-\frac{B_T}{2}(a_0-\Psi_0^{1/2}/B_T)^2}\,da_0 \Big/ \int g(a_0)e^{-\frac{B_T}{2}(a_0-\Psi_0^{1/2}/B_T)^2}\,da_0 \tag{3.56}$$

where $g(a_0) \cong \sigma(a_0)/\sqrt{a_0}$. From the above it is clear that if the processing gains ($\sim\Phi_s, B_T$) are sufficiently large and if $\sigma(a_0)$ and $g(a_0)$

† Ref. 6, pp. 373–380 and 389–391.

‡ Here and in the rest of this section we abbreviate $(\Phi_T)_s$ by Φ_s [cf. Eqs. (2.51)] for continuous sampling on $(0,T)$.

are suitably smooth and not too small at and near $a_0 = \Phi_v/\Phi_s$ or $\Psi_0^{1/2}/B_T$, then the significant contributions to the integrals occur essentially at and about these values of a_0. In fact, as Φ_s (and B_T) $\to \infty$, it can be shown that the estimators

$$a^*_{\text{QCF}}\Big|_{\text{coh}} \simeq \Phi_v/\Phi_s \equiv z_0 \qquad a^*_{\text{QCF}}\Big|_{\text{incoh}} \simeq \Psi_0^{1/2}/B_T \equiv x_0 \quad (3.57)$$

are asymptotically optimum and canonical in the above sense.† Thus, for practical purposes, *these limiting Bayes estimators are independent of almost all reasonable a priori distributions and choices of error function.* Specific necessary and sufficient conditions for this to be so are given in Ref. 6.‡

Other interesting properties of the canonical estimators a_0^* [Eq. (3.57)] follow: The conditional d.d.'s of $a_0^*(z_0)$, $a_0^*(x_0)$ are readily found to be

$$W_1(a_0^*(z_0)|a_0) = \sqrt{\frac{\Phi_s}{2\pi}}\, e^{-\frac{1}{2}\Phi_s(a_0^*-a_0)^2} \quad (3.58)$$

$$W_1(a_0^*(x_0)|a_0) = B_T a_0^* e^{-a_0^{*2}B_T/2 - a_0^2 B_T/2} I_0(a_0 a_0^* B_T) \qquad a_0^* \geq 0 \quad (3.59)$$

from which one can show directly that in either instance

$$W_1(a_0^*) = \sigma(a_0^*) \quad (3.60)$$

namely, *the unconditional d.d. of the canonical Bayes estimators* a_0^*($= z_0$, or x_0) *is simply the a priori d.d. of amplitude, with* a_0 *replaced by* a_0^*. Applying Eqs. (3.58) and (3.59) to Eq. (3.4) for interval estimation, one obtains the canonical forms

$$P[(1-\lambda)a_0 \leq a_0^*(x_0), a_0^*(z_0) \leq (1+\lambda)a_0] = \int_{(1-\lambda)a_0}^{(1+\lambda)a_0} W_0(a_0^*|a_0)\, da_0^*$$
$$= \Theta(\lambda\sigma_0) \quad (3.61)$$

where $\sigma_0^2 = a_0^2\Phi_s/2$, or $a_0^2 B_T/2$, is the familiar output signal-to-noise ratio; cf. Eqs. (2.48) and (2.64). Figure 3.1 also applies here for the present canonical result (3.61). With white noise backgrounds Eq. (3.20), ($\sigma_A^2 \to \infty$), applies for $A^*_{0\text{-coh}}$ and Eq. (3.53) for $A^*_{0\text{-incoh}}$, respectively, from Eq. (3.57), while σ_0^2 becomes E_s/W_0 once more; cf. Eqs. (2.54) and (2.70), with appropriate modifications of Eqs. (3.58) and (3.59).§

† Ref. 6, pp. 374 and 375.
‡ *Ibid.*
§ Thus $W_1(A_0^*|A_0) = W_1(a_0^*|a_0)|\, da_0^*/dA_0^*|$, with $A_0^* = \sqrt{2\psi}\, a_0^*$, etc.

Some other properties of the limiting, canonical estimators (3.57) are

1. $a_0^* = z_0, x_0$, are asymptotically Minimax.
2. z_0, x_0 converge mean-square (MSC) and in probability (CIP),† i.e., $\lim_{BT\to\infty} E_{v|a_0}\{|a_0 - a_0^*|^2\} = 0.$
3. The a_0^* are unbiased, e.g., $E_{v,a_0}\{a_0^*\} = \overline{a_0}$.

Although these relations are also invariant of a priori distribution and choice of cost function, the associated Bayes errors are not. In practical circumstances we may use these limiting, canonical forms (3.57) even when the processing gain, or the output signal-to-noise ratio σ_0^2, are only large compared to unity and not infinite. A more detailed study of these optimum estimators in their approach to the limiting, canonical state reveals that

$$a_{0\text{-opt}}^* \simeq (z_0 \text{ or } x_0) + (b_{\text{coh}} \text{ or } b_{\text{incoh}}) \tag{3.62}$$

where b_{coh}, etc., are constants *dependent now on the cost function and a priori d.d.* The departures of the interval estimates, optimum structure, Bayes error, etc., for Eq. (3.62) from those determined from the strictly canonical forms z_0, x_0, however, are usually small enough to permit the latter's use for values of σ_0^2 as low as 8 to 10 db, while $\sigma_0^2 \geq 13$ db is usually more than sufficient for safe application.

The comparative simplicity and explicitness of the theory of amplitude estimation outlined in this section and in Secs. 3.3 and 3.4 is attributable basically to (1) the fact that the quantity being estimated, viz., amplitude, appears *linearly* in the available data [cf. Eq. (3.18)] and to (2) the fact that the accompanying noise is normal. However, from these examples one should not infer comparable simplicity and explicitness, even with normal noise backgrounds, for the wider variety of problems where the signal parameter (or parameters) to be estimated appear *nonlinearly* in the received data. The measurement of range, velocity, and acceleration from radar or sonar signals are cases in point. Nevertheless, when the output (i.e., processed) signal is strong, which is the situation of usual interest anyway, perturbation methods can be employed that yield useful estimates of the desired parameters and the associated statistical errors, when both QCF and SCF (maximum likelihood) criteria are chosen.[7,8] The success of these methods and the quasi-canonical results that stem from them depend, of course, on

† Ref. 1, pp. 65 and 66.

strong processed signals, so that adequate processing techniques provide good estimates at the outset and the errors are on the average small compared with these estimates. Further treatment of problems of this type may be found in Ref. 1, secs. 21.1 and 22.3 and the references listed in chap. 21; in Ref. 9, chap. 14; and in Ref. 10, chap. 8.

References

1. Middleton, D.: "An Introduction to Statistical Communication Theory," McGraw-Hill Book Company, New York, 1960.
2. Wiener, N.: "Extrapolation, Interpolation, and Smoothing of Stationary Time Series," The Technology Press of the Massachusetts Institute of Technology, Cambridge, Mass., and John Wiley & Sons, Inc., New York, 1949.
3. Kolmogoroff, A. N.: Interpolation and Extrapolation, *Bull. Acad. Sci. USSR, Math. Ser.*, **5**:3–14 (1944).
4. Middleton, D.: Optimization Problems in Statistical Communication Theory, in R. Bellman (ed.): "Mathematical Optimization Techniques," chap. 7, University of California Press, Berkeley, Calif., 1963.
5. Bellman, R., R. E. Kalaba, and D. Middleton: Dynamic Programming, Sequential Estimation, and Sequential Detection Processes, *Proc. Nat. Acad. Sci. U.S.*, **47**(3):338–341 (1961).
6. Middleton, D.: The Incoherent Estimation of Signal Amplitudes in Normal Noise Backgrounds, in M. Rosenblatt (ed.): "Time Series Analysis," chap. 24, John Wiley & Sons, Inc., New York, 1963.
7. Kelly, E. J., I. S. Reed, and W. L. Root: The Detection of Radar Echoes in Noise: I, *J. Soc. Ind. Appl. Math.* **8**(2):309–341 (1960); see in particular for extraction problems *ibid.*, II, **8**(3):481–507 (1960).
8. Swerling, P.: Parameter Estimation Accuracy Formulas, *IEEE, Trans. Inform. Theory.* **IT-10,** No. 4, Oct. 1964.
9. Davenport, W. B., Jr., and W. L. Root: "Introduction to the Theory of Random Signals and Noise," McGraw-Hill Book Company, New York, 1958.
10. Wainstein, L. A., and V. D. Zubakov: "Extraction of Signals from Noise," trans. by R. A Silverman, Prentice-Hall, Inc., Englewood Cliffs, N.J., 1962.

Chapter 4

The Structure of Optimum Systems

For the Bayes receivers $T_{R\text{-opt}}^{(N)}$ treated in this study, optimum structure is embodied in the decision rules δ^* (cf. Sec. 1.3). As we have already observed in Chap. 2, the optimum decision rule in the case of detection reduces to the calculation of a likelihood ratio Λ, which is compared to a threshold for a definite decision [cf. (2.25)]. On the other hand, we have noted in Chap. 3 that for signal extraction δ^* becomes the optimum estimator γ^*, whose explicit form also depends on the choice of cost function. In general, for detection we find on combining (2.27) and (2.33) with (2.35) that δ^* is explicitly

$$\delta^*(\gamma_0^*|\mathbf{V}) = \int_{-\infty}^{\log \mathcal{K}_{01}} \delta[x - \log \Lambda_n(\mathbf{V})]\, dx$$

$$\delta^*(\gamma_1^*|\mathbf{V}) = \int_{\log \mathcal{K}_{01}}^{\infty} \delta[x - \log \Lambda_n(\mathbf{V})]\, dx$$

while for extraction we have $\delta^*(\gamma^*|\mathbf{V}) = \delta(\gamma - \gamma_\sigma^*(\mathbf{V}))$ [cf. Eq. (3.1)]. These decision rules represent *different* functions (or functionals) of the a priori d.d. $F_n(\mathbf{V}|\mathbf{S})$ of the received data V, mainly because of the different cost functions involved. Both Λ and γ^* are usually nonlinear functions (or functionals) of the received data. The optimum detectors of Secs. 2.5 and 2.6 and the optimum estimators of Secs. 3.3 to 3.5 are typical examples of such linear and nonlinear operations.

However, it is not enough for the system designer to rest upon such purely analytical, representations. He faces the essential task of resolving these mathematical forms into ordered sequences of operators, each of which has its physical counterpart in terms of physically realizable† elements. When this has been accomplished, the details of the instrumentation can normally be carried out in a great variety of ways, appropriate to the particular application at hand. The purpose of the present chapter is to show how, at least in the critical situation of threshold reception,‡ the structure of these optimum receivers may be so resolved.[1–3]

4.1 *Structure for Threshold Reception*

In Sec. 2.7 a canonical, locally Bayes theory of threshold detection has been outlined which is broadly independent of the statistical properties of signal and noise and their mode of combination. One has in the on-off binary cases specifically

$$\hat{\mathbf{T}}_{R\text{-opt}}^{(N)}\{\mathbf{V}\} = \log \mu + \hat{B}_n(\theta) + \theta \left(\frac{\partial \log \Lambda_n(\mathbf{V}|\theta)}{\partial \theta} \right)_{\theta=0} \tag{4.1}$$

where the parameter θ is a measure of the input signal-to-noise ratio for this optimum receiver [cf. Eqs. (2.74) et seq.]. The explicit structure depends, of course, on the form of the derivative, and until this is given we can go no further toward a structural description. However, with *additive* noise processes, further development is possible; canonical results here are given by Eqs. (2.75) to (2.77), although the explicit dependence of $\hat{T}_{R\text{-opt}}^{(N)}$ on $\mathbf{V}$ [or on $V(t)$ in the continuous cases] is still concealed; cf. Eqs. (2.76). A further expansion leads to the author's original development [Ref. 1, eq. (19.45) et seq.], which yields the required explicit dependence on the received data; cf. Eqs. (2.79) and comments. Cross correlations and autocorrelations involving V and S now appear to all orders in V.

In our present discussion we shall consider only terms of the first and

† Physical realizability here is the requirement of *causality*, namely, that the element (or system) cannot operate on the "future" of its input.

‡ See the first footnote on p. 45 and the paragraph following Eq. (3.39).

second orders, i.e., terms linear and quadratic in **V**. Apart from the complexity of the higher-order terms, which makes it desirable to omit them whenever possible, we further limit the treatment to additive, *normal* noise backgrounds, which at once greatly simplifies the development of (log) Λ_n; in fact, it eliminates all higher products in **V** in (4.1) above. Thus, from Eqs. (2.79) with Eq. (2.40)† for the noise, we see at once that

$$\mathbf{y} = -\mathbf{k}_N^{-1}\bar{\mathbf{v}}_N + \mathbf{k}_N^{-1}\mathbf{v} \qquad \mathbf{z} = -\mathbf{k}_N^{-1} \tag{4.2}$$

precisely, so that the optimum threshold detectors for coherent and incoherent reception are now from Eqs. (2.77)

$$\hat{x}\Big|_{\text{coh}} = \log\mu + [B_n^{(c)}(\theta_c) - \theta_c\tilde{\bar{\mathbf{v}}}_N\mathbf{k}_N^{-1}\bar{\mathbf{s}}'] + \theta_c\tilde{\mathbf{v}}\mathbf{k}_N^{-1}\bar{\mathbf{s}}'$$
$$\theta_c\bar{\mathbf{s}}' = \overline{a_0\mathbf{s}} = \bar{a}_0\bar{\mathbf{s}} \tag{4.3}$$

$$\hat{x}\Big|_{\text{incoh}} = \log\mu + \left[B_n^{(I)}(\theta_I) - \frac{\theta_I}{2}\,\text{trace}\,\boldsymbol{\varrho}\mathbf{k}_N^{-1}\right]$$
$$+ \tfrac{1}{2}\theta_I(\tilde{\mathbf{v}} - \tilde{\bar{\mathbf{v}}}_N)\mathbf{k}_N^{-1}\boldsymbol{\varrho}\mathbf{k}_N^{-1}(\mathbf{v} - \bar{\mathbf{v}}_N) \qquad \begin{cases} \bar{\mathbf{s}} = 0 \\ \boldsymbol{\varrho} \equiv \mathbf{k}_S = \overline{\mathbf{s}\tilde{\mathbf{s}}} \end{cases} \tag{4.4}$$

respectively,‡ with $\theta_c = \sqrt{\overline{a_0^2}} = \sqrt{\theta_I}$. Note that $\hat{x}\big|_{\text{incoh}}$ contains both linear and quadratic terms (unless $\bar{\mathbf{v}}_N = 0$, which is frequently the case), for we can rewrite Eq. (4.4) as:

$$\hat{x}\Big|_{\text{incoh}} = \log\mu + \left[B_n^{(I)}(\theta_I) + \frac{\theta_I}{2}\,\tilde{\bar{\mathbf{v}}}_N(\mathbf{k}_N^{-1}\mathbf{k}_S\mathbf{k}_N^{-1})\bar{\mathbf{v}}_N - \frac{\theta_I}{2}\,\text{trace}\,\mathbf{k}_S\mathbf{k}_N^{-1}\right]$$
$$- \theta_I\tilde{\mathbf{v}}(\mathbf{k}_N^{-1}\mathbf{k}_S\mathbf{k}_N^{-1})\bar{\mathbf{v}}_N + \frac{\theta_I}{2}\,\tilde{\mathbf{v}}(\mathbf{k}_N^{-1}\mathbf{k}_S\mathbf{k}_N^{-1})\mathbf{v} \tag{4.4a}$$

showing also the additional contributions to the bias, [ ]. More compactly still, we may express Eqs. (4.3) and 4.4) as

$$\hat{x}\Big|_{\text{coh}} = B_0' + \theta_c B_1'\tilde{\mathbf{v}}\mathbf{C}\bar{\mathbf{s}}'$$
$$\hat{x}\Big|_{\text{incoh}} = B_0'' + \theta_I B_1''\tilde{\mathbf{v}}\mathbf{G}\bar{\mathbf{v}}_N + \theta_I B_2''\tilde{\mathbf{v}}\mathbf{G}\mathbf{v} \tag{4.5}$$

where **C** and **G**, B_0', etc., are at once identified on comparing Eqs. (4.5) with Eqs. (4.3) and (4.4). We emphasize again that the structures in

† In which **v** is replaced by $\mathbf{v} - \bar{\mathbf{v}}_N$, $\bar{\mathbf{v}}_N \neq 0$, to account for possible nonzero means. One has the usual normalization $\bar{\mathbf{v}}_N = \psi_N^{-1/2}\bar{\mathbf{V}}_N$ and $\bar{\mathbf{V}}_N = \bar{\mathbf{N}}$ for noise alone.

‡ We make the usually unrestrictive assumption that amplitude and waveform are statistically independent; cf. Eq. (4.3).

(4.5) are not restricted to deterministic signals alone but may apply equally for those signals that are entirely stochastic (and not necessarily gaussian), stationary or nonstationary, and broad- or narrow-band.

An alternative form of $\hat{x}\Big|_{\text{incoh}}$ that is convenient when the signals involved are narrow-band and deterministic (and when $\bar{\mathbf{v}}_N = 0$) may be derived from the author's earlier result based on the narrow-band assumption,† viz.,

$$\begin{aligned}(T^{(N)}_{R\text{-opt}})_{\text{det}}\{V\} &= \log \Lambda_n(\mathbf{V}|\boldsymbol{\theta}) \\ &= \log \mu + \log \langle e^{-a_0{}^2 B_n(\boldsymbol{\theta})/2} I_0(a_0 \sqrt{\Psi_0(\boldsymbol{\theta})})\rangle_{a_0,\boldsymbol{\theta}} \qquad (4.6)\end{aligned}$$

where $\boldsymbol{\theta}$ represents all other random parameters of the signal; $B_n(\boldsymbol{\theta})$, $\Psi_0(\boldsymbol{\theta}) \equiv \tilde{\mathbf{v}}\mathbf{G}_0(\boldsymbol{\theta})\mathbf{v}$ are the discrete versions‡ of B_T, Ψ_0 respectively defined in Eqs. (2.58*a*) and (2.58*b*) for continuous sampling, and $\theta_I = \overline{a_0^2}$ once more. The locally optimum Bayes detector $\hat{x}\Big|_{\text{incoh}}$ is easily found from Eq. (4.6) in Eq. (4.1) to be

$$\hat{x}\Big|_{\text{incoh}} = \log \mu + \left[B_n^{(I)}(\theta_I) - \frac{\theta_I}{2}\overline{B_n(\boldsymbol{\theta})}\right] + \frac{\theta_I}{4}\overline{\tilde{\mathbf{v}}\mathbf{G}_0(\boldsymbol{\theta})\mathbf{v}} \qquad \theta_I = \overline{a_0^2} \qquad (4.7)$$

which reduces as expected to Eq. (4.4*a*), with $\bar{\mathbf{v}}_N = 0$, since $\mathbf{G}_0 \doteq 2\mathbf{G}$ and trace $\mathbf{k}_S\mathbf{k}_N^{-1} \doteq B_n(\boldsymbol{\theta})$ under the narrow-band approximation.§

Finally, we mention the comparatively rare cases where an explicit, *exact* detector structure for all signal levels can be found; three examples are discussed in Secs. 2.5 and 2.6. From Eqs. (2.43), (2.59), and (2.65) these optimum structures are

coherent:

$$x = \log \mu - \frac{a_0^2}{2}\tilde{\mathbf{s}}\mathbf{k}_N^{-1}\mathbf{s} + a_0\tilde{\mathbf{v}}\mathbf{k}_N^{-1}\mathbf{s} \qquad (4.8a)$$

incoherent:

$$z = a_0^2\Psi_0 \qquad \Psi_0 \equiv \tilde{\mathbf{v}}\mathbf{G}_0\mathbf{v} \qquad (4.8b)$$

incoherent:

$$y_R = \log \mu - \log(1 + \sigma_R^2) + \frac{\overline{a_0^2}\Psi_0}{4(1 + \sigma_R^2)} \qquad \sigma_R^2 = \overline{a_0^2}B_T/2 \qquad (4.8c)$$

† Ref. 2, sec. 20.1-3, eq. (20.31).
‡ Ref. 2, eqs. (20.26) and (20.29) and pp. 845–847.
§ *Ibid.*

respectively for (1) the optimum detection of deterministic signals known exactly; (2) (narrow-band) signals known exactly except for RF epoch; and (3) (narrow-band) signals known exactly except for RF epoch while subject to slow Rayleigh fading, all three types of signal observed in additive normal noise. These structures likewise have the characteristic forms of $\hat{x}_{\text{coh}}$ and $\hat{x}_{\text{incoh}}$ [cf. Eqs. (4.5)], requiring only linear and quadratic operations on the received data.

Even under the rather loose restriction of additive signal and noise a corresponding canonical theory for optimum threshold extraction is not so easily constructed. For although the criterion of optimality is still minimization of average risk (or error), a much broader class of cost (or error) function is now possible. This in effect provides an additional degree of freedom for the designer and noticeably affects the explicit form of the resulting Bayes estimators γ^*. An important exception where a canonical theory is possible is the optimum estimation of the amplitudes of deterministic signals under certain conditions, as we have noted in Sec. 3.5. For coherent and incoherent reception in normal noise the limiting canonical structures are found to be [cf. Eqs. (3.57)]

coherent:

$$z_0 = \tilde{\mathbf{v}}\mathbf{k}_N^{-1}\mathbf{s}/\tilde{\mathbf{s}}\mathbf{k}_N^{-1}\mathbf{s} \tag{4.9a}$$

incoherent:

$$x_0 = \Psi_0^{1/2}/B_n \tag{4.9b}$$

(with $\tilde{\mathbf{s}}\mathbf{k}_N^{-1}\mathbf{s} \to (\Phi_T)_s$, $B_n \to B_T$, etc., for continuous sampling, in the usual way). However, although we cannot expect such comparatively simple results for general estimators, we can seek once more suitable approximations based only on linear and quadratic operations on the data, or at most on computable functions of such operations [e.g., $\Psi_0^{1/2}$, or ${}_1F_1(1/2; 1; -\Psi_0/2B_T)^{-1}$; cf. Eq. (3.41)].

Accordingly, from the above it is evident that optimum threshold structure can be expressed in terms of the fundamental components of linear and quadratic operations on the received data, of the form

$$\Phi_n \equiv \tilde{\mathbf{v}}\mathbf{C}^{(1)}\mathbf{g} \qquad \text{and} \qquad \Psi_n \equiv \tilde{\mathbf{v}}\mathbf{G}^{(2)}\mathbf{v} \tag{4.10}$$

where positive definiteness (and sometimes symmetry) of $\mathbf{C}$ and $\mathbf{G}$ are sufficient conditions for the realization of these operations. With continuous sampling on $(0,T)$ these relations go over into

$$\Phi_T(v) = \psi \iint_T v(t)G^{(1)}(t,u)g(u)\,dt\,du$$
$$\Psi_T(v) = \psi \iint_T v(t)G^{(2)}(t,u)v(u)\,dt\,du \qquad (4.11)$$
$$\psi = \overline{N^2}$$

with $v(t) = V(t)/\sqrt{\psi}$, in which the $G^{(1),(2)}$ are determined from the solutions of certain integral equations† (cf. the Appendix). Our task now is to show how these quadratic structure elements can be resolved into ordered sequences of realizable operations on the input data V. For this we shall follow the approach of a recent paper.[1]

4.2 *Linear Operations: Bayes Matched Filters of the First Kind*[1]

Let us begin by considering first the general concept of a *matched filter*,‡,[5–7] which we shall need in the resolution of structure, as typified by the linear and nonlinear operations embodied in the quadratic forms of Eqs. (4.10) and (4.11). "Matching" is a form of optimization which attempts to enhance in some appropriate sense the reception of a desired signal in the undesired noise background. As we have noted earlier, reception may involve either a detection or an extraction process (or both). Matched filters here, as in earlier work, are required to be linear (but not necessarily time-invariant) and may be used in conjunction with other, subsequent zero-memory nonlinear elements and "postdetection," linear integrating devices. However, in contrast to earlier definitions, our present definition of a matched filter is more general and includes the earlier examples as special cases, as we shall see below.

The structure of matched filters depends on (1) the nature of the signal; (2) the statistics of the accompanying noise, and the way in which it combines with the signal; and (3) in particular on the criterion of optimality which is chosen. Since (1) and (2) are essentially a priori data, it is (3), the choice of criterion, that permits an extension of the earlier definitions. The latter have all been based on energy calculations, i.e., on some form of maximization of signal energy vis-à-vis that

† Ref. 2, sec. 19.4-2.
‡ Ref. 1, and for other earlier work, refs. 3–11 listed therein; Ref. 2, sec. 16.3. See also Ref. 7, chap. 3, and *IRE, Trans. Inform. Theory*, **IT-6**:(3) (1960).

of the noise, without direct reference to the actual decision process implied in reception. Usually, these matched filters have been obtained by maximizing a signal-to-noise ratio and may thus be called S/N matched filters. By recognizing that reception here implies a definite decision process, we can extend this matched filter concept, basing it on the Bayes decision rules considered previously in Chaps. 1 to 3. When this is done, such optimum (linear) filters are called *Bayes matched filters*, whose precise structure, of course, depends on the properties of signal and noise, as well as on the decision criterion, which generates characteristic structural components of the types (4.10) and (4.11).

Consider now the linear operation embodied in the quadratic form $\tilde{\mathbf{v}}\mathbf{C}^{(1)}\mathbf{g}$ [cf. (4.10)] when $\mathbf{C}^{(1)}$ is symmetrical. A number of structural interpretations are possible; we begin by writing

$$\mathbf{v}_F = \mathbf{Q}_c\mathbf{v} \tag{4.12}$$

for the discretely filtered wave on $(0,T)$, obtained by passing normalized data $\mathbf{v}$ through a (discrete) Bayes matched filter $\mathbf{Q}_c = \mathbf{C}^{(1)}$, which also truncates the input to ensure finite samples on the finite interval $(0,T)$. We have directly

$$\Phi_n = \tilde{\mathbf{v}}_F\mathbf{g} = \sum_{j=1}^{n} v_F(t_j)g(t_j) \tag{4.13}$$

The result is a discrete cross correlation, without delay (i.e., multiplication) of the filtered input with the (locally available) $\mathbf{g}$. We see that the linear operation $\mathbf{Q}_c = \mathbf{C}^{(1)}$ assumes the role of a Bayes matched filter, which may or may not be invariant and realizable.†

The matched filter $\mathbf{Q}_c$ may be written in more detail in terms of a (truncated) weighting function h_c:

$$\begin{aligned}\mathbf{C}^{(1)} = \mathbf{Q}_c = [H_c(t_i,t_j)\,\Delta t] &= [h_c(t_i - t_j,\, t_i)\,\Delta t] \\ &= [\hat{h}_c(t_i,\, t_i - t_j)\,\Delta t] = \tilde{\mathbf{C}}^{(1)}\end{aligned} \tag{4.14}$$

since $\mathbf{C}^{(1)}$ is symmetrical‡ and thus exhibits the time-varying character of the weighting function. Realizability is expressed by the condition

$$H_c(t_i,t_j) = h_c(t_i - t_j,\, t_i) = 0 \qquad t_j > t_i \tag{4.15}$$

† Usually, if we invoke invariance, we do so at the expense of realizability, and vice versa.

‡ We can always write $A(x,y) = C(x - y,\, x)$, if $A(x,y) = A(y,x)$; cf. ref. 31 in Ref. 1.

However, we cannot impose this condition on Φ_n without changing its value, since $v_i g_j C_{ij}^{(1)} \neq v_j g_i C_{ji}^{(1)}$. The time-varying filter h_c (or $\mathbf{Q}_c$) is thus not realizable because of the unsymmetrical nature of Φ_n itself. Note, as well, that if h_c is invariant, i.e., $h_c(t_i,t_j) = h_c(|t_i - t_j|)$, realizability is still not possible, since $h_c \neq 0$, $t_i > t_j$ [cf. Eq. (4.15)].

Another interpretation of Φ_n is possible, nevertheless, which does use a realizable matched filter. To see this, let $\boldsymbol{\lambda}$ be a column vector, such that

$$\mathbf{C}^{(1)}\mathbf{g} = \boldsymbol{\lambda} \tag{4.16}$$

Then Eq. (4.13) becomes

$$\Phi_n = \tilde{\mathbf{v}}\boldsymbol{\lambda} = \sum_{j=1}^{n} v(t_j)\lambda_j \tag{4.17}$$

Next, we set

$$\boldsymbol{\lambda} = [h_M(T - t_j)\,\Delta t] \tag{4.18}$$

where h_M is the weighting function of a time-invariant realizable linear filter, with a readout time $T(= n\,\Delta t)$, so that

$$\Phi_n = \sum_{j=1}^{n} v(t_j)h_M(T - t_j)\,\Delta t \tag{4.19}$$

showing that Φ_n is the output of this discrete, realizable, invariant Bayes matched filter at time $t = T$ when $\mathbf{v}$ is the input. Such filters are realized in practice by a delay-line filter with suitable weighting and readout at $t = T$. From Eqs. (4.12) to (4.14) and (4.16) it is evident that $\mathbf{Q}_c$ is related to $h_M\,\Delta t$ by $\boldsymbol{\lambda} = \mathbf{Q}_c\mathbf{g}$. The Bayes filter h_M is closely related to, and in some cases identical with, the S/N matched filters of the earlier theory.[5,6]

With continuous sampling, the functional $\Phi_T(v)$, [Eqs. (4.11)] becomes

$$\Phi_T(v) = \int_{0-}^{T+} V(t)h_M(T - t)\,dt$$
$$\text{with} \qquad h_M(T - t) \equiv \sqrt{\psi}\int_{0-}^{T+} G^{(1)}(t,u)g(u)\,du \tag{4.20}$$

where $h_M = 0$ outside $(0-,T+)$. Again, the (now continuous) matched filter h_M is invariant and realizable, with readout at $t = T$. Similarly, the continuous version of Eqs. (4.12) to (4.14) is

$$\Phi_T(v) = \int_{0-}^{T+} V_F(t)g(t)\,dt$$
$$\text{with} \qquad V_F(t) \equiv \sqrt{\psi}\int_{0-}^{T+} V(u)H_c(t,u)\,du \tag{4.21}$$

where now $G^{(1)} = H_c(t,u)$ [cf. Eq. (4.15)]; however, $H_c(t,u)$ is not realizable. Usually, h_M is simpler to implement than H_c.

In the important special case where the background noise is white, with spectral density W_0, and $g(t) = s(t)$, a normalized signal [cf. Eqs. (2.42) and (4.8*a*), for example], one can show that†

$$G^{(1)}(t,u) = H_c(t,u) = (2/W_0)\delta(t-u), \quad (t\epsilon T)$$

and therefore from Eq. (4.20) that $h_M(T-t) = 2s(t)/W_0$, $(t\epsilon T)$, with

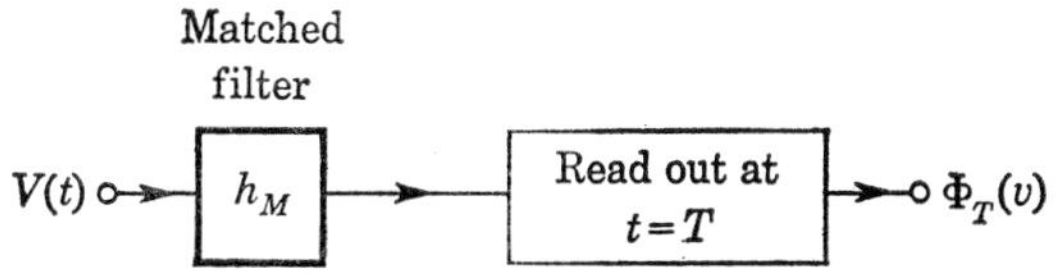

Fig. 4.1 Resolution of $\Phi_T(v)$ by a Bayes matched filter (h_M) of the first kind, type 1. (Realizable.)

$V_F(t) = 2V(t)/W_0$. Observe that when $V(t) = S(t) + N(t)$ we can write with this matched filter

$$a_0\Phi_T(v)\Big|_{\text{white}} = \frac{A_0}{\sqrt{2}}\int_0^T V(t)\left[\frac{2}{W_0}s(t)\right]dt$$

$$\doteq \frac{2}{W_0}\int_0^T S(t)^2\,dt = 2(S/N)^2_{\text{out}} \qquad \text{[Eq. (2.53)]} \quad (4.22)$$

since $\overline{N} = 0$, the noise is white, and $S = a_0\sqrt{\psi}\,s$ from Eq. (2.42). The matched filter h_M with readout at $t' = T$ gives us the maximum of the correlation function $W_0^{-1}\int_0^T S(t)S(t+t'-T)\,dt$ [$\sim(S/N)^2_{\text{out}}$, Eq. (2.53)] and is thus a special case of a *correlation filter*, or *correlator*.‡ This filter also maximizes the output signal-to-noise ratio in the earlier sense of an (S/N) matched filter and, in fact, is identical with it here. Generally, we call $h_M(T-t)$ and $H_c(t,u)$, along with their discrete counterparts (4.15) and (4.18), *Bayes matched filters of the first kind, types 1 and 2*, respectively.§ Figures 4.1 and 4.2 show these two equivalent realizations of the linear functional $\Phi_T(v)$, with obvious modifications for the discrete cases.

† Ref. 2, eqs. (20.43*a*) and (20.43*b*).
‡ Ref. 7, sec. 17.
§ This is a somewhat different classification from that originally employed in Refs. 1 and 2 (cf. sec. 20.2-4 in Ref. 2).

Finally, we may mention still another important special case of the Bayes matched filter of the first kind, type 1, which is also identical with the corresponding special form of the S/N matched filter. This is the so-called *inverse filter*,† which occurs when (1) the accompanying noise consists of a "clutter" component, whose spectral intensity density is proportional to that of the illuminating signal $|S(f)|^2$, e.g.,

$$\mathcal{W}_c(f) = \gamma_0|S(f)|^2$$

and an additive background or system noise component $\mathcal{W}_{N_0}(f)$ that is weak vis-à-vis the clutter term, and (2) when the observation time T is

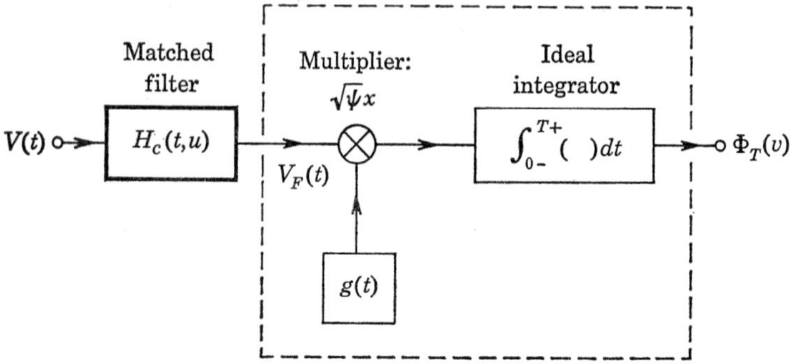

Fig. 4.2 Resolution of $\Phi_T(v)$ by a Bayes matched filter (H_c) of the first kind, type 2. (Nonrealizable.)

sufficiently long with respect to the correlation time of the noise to be regarded as essentially infinite. Thus, for example, we can use the results of sec. 16.3-2(3) in Ref. 2 to write for the system function $Y_M(i\omega)$ $(= \mathfrak{F}\{h_M\})$ of our matched filter in white noise and clutter in this limiting situation

$$Y_M(i\omega) = \frac{2k_0S(f)^*}{W_0 + \gamma_0|S(f)|^2} \tag{4.22a}$$

when k_0 is an adjustable (complex) scale factor.

For strong signals and hence strong clutter, we have $\mathcal{W}_c \gg W_0$, and Eq. (4.22*a*) therefore becomes

$$Y_M(i\omega) \doteq \frac{2k_0}{\gamma_0} S(f)^{-1} \tag{4.22b}$$

† Ref. 7, sec. 21.

which is the aforementioned inverse filter, also maximizing $(S/N)^2_{\text{out}}$ [cf. Eq. (4.22)] under these circumstances. Note, on the other hand, that when the clutter is weak or nonexistent, we get

$$Y_M(i\omega) = 2k_0 S(f)^*/W_0$$

which is just (the Fourier transform of) the familiar form of h_M above. We may describe this behavior in more detail by observing that with strong signals of fixed power and not too large a bandwidth, the inverse filter (4.22*b*) is the desired optimum form. As the signal spectrum is broadened, its intensity falls, while the clutter return exhibits a progressively finer structure in time. For example, if the signal consists of a very short pulse or a train of such short pulses (as in radar applications, for instance), the clutter may be resolved into individual returns, with little or no overlapping in time, and with a consequent improvement in signal detection and resolution of desired targets. However, although progressive shortening of the emitted pulses improves resolution, the point is eventually reached where the clutter component is dominated by the white noise background, subclutter visibility is lost, and the appropriate matched filter is once more the correlation filter h_M of the earlier theory.

4.3 *Quadratic Operations: Bayes Matched Filters of the Second Kind*†

When the basic operations on the input data are nonlinear, as typified by the quadratic forms of Eqs. (4.10) and (4.11), the resolution into realizable elements is more involved. As before, let us begin with the discrete cases and consider a first type of matched filter embodied in Ψ_n and Ψ_T. These are linear filters followed by zero-memory square-law devices and ideal integration. To see this we first introduce in Eq. (4.10) a (real) linear discrete filter $\mathbf{Q}[\neq \mathbf{Q}_c$; cf. Eq. (4.12)], once more with truncation on $(0,T)$, such that

$$\mathbf{v}_F = \mathbf{Q}\mathbf{v}$$

and therefore $$\Psi_n = \tilde{\mathbf{v}}_F \tilde{\mathbf{Q}}^{-1}\mathbf{C}^{(2)}\mathbf{Q}^{-1}\mathbf{v}_F \ (>0) \tag{4.23}$$

where $\mathbf{v}_F$ is this filter's output. Because $\mathbf{C}^{(2)}$ is required to be symmetrical and positive-definite here, with $[C_{ij}^{(2)} = 0;\ i,j > n,\ i,j < 1$, etc., since only finite data samples are treated] we observe that it is always possible to find a congruent transformation $\mathbf{Q}$ which simultaneously

† Ref. 1, pp. 353 and 354.

diagonalizes $\mathbf{C}^{(2)}$ and reduces it to the unit matrix, viz.,

$$\mathbf{C}^{(2)} = \tilde{\mathbf{Q}}\mathbf{Q} \qquad 1 \le i,j \le n$$
$$= 0 \qquad \text{other } (i,j) \tag{4.24}$$

Thus we have
$$\Psi_n = \tilde{\mathbf{v}}_F \mathbf{v}_F = \sum_{j=1}^{n} v_F^2(t_j) \tag{4.25}$$

which is a zero-memory square-law operation on the *filtered* wave v_F, followed by an ideal integration (here, summation) over the data in the period $(0,T)$.

The discrete filter $\mathbf{Q}$ is called a (discrete) Bayes matched filter of the *second kind, type* 1. Its properties are readily summarized:

1. $\mathbf{Q}$ is *linear* [cf. Eqs. (4.23)].
2. $\mathbf{Q}_{ij} = 0$; $j > i$, which expresses the fact that $\mathbf{C}^{(2)}$ may be reduced to diagonal form by a congruent transformation with this property.† Thus, $\mathbf{Q}$ represents a *realizable* filter, e.g.,

$$\mathbf{Q} \equiv [H(t_i,t_j)\,\Delta t] = [h(t_i - t_j,\, t_i)\,\Delta t] = 0 \qquad t_j > t_i \qquad \tilde{\mathbf{Q}} \ne \mathbf{Q} \tag{4.26}$$

3. Therefore $\mathbf{Q} = [h(t_i - t_j,\, t_i)\,\Delta t]$, all t_i, t_j (where $\mathbf{Q} \ne 0$) is *time-varying*.

It is convenient to set

$$\mathbf{C}^{(2)} \equiv [\rho_c(t_i,t_j)\,\Delta t] = [\rho_c(t_j,t_i)\,\Delta t] = \boldsymbol{\varrho}_c\,\Delta t \tag{4.27}$$

where we recall from Eq. (4.24) that $\boldsymbol{\varrho}_c = 0$ outside $(1 \le i,j \le n)$, since only operations on data acquired in $(0,T)$ are used in the decision process. The set of basic nonlinear equations determining the elements of $\mathbf{Q}$ can be equivalently expressed as

$$\rho_c(t_i,t_j) = \sum_{l=1}^{n} h(t_l - t_i,\, t_l)h(t_l - t_j,\, t_l)\,\Delta t \qquad 1 \le i,j \le n$$
$$= 0 \qquad \text{elsewhere} \tag{4.28}$$

and the quadratic form Ψ_n becomes accordingly

$$\Psi_n = \sum_{j=1}^{n} \Big(\sum_{i=1}^{\infty\,(\text{or } j)} v(t_i)h(t_j - t_i,\, t_j)\,\Delta t \Big)^2 = \sum_{j=1}^{n} v_F(t_j)^2 \tag{4.29}$$

which gives as one interpretation of structure the sequence of a real-

† See Ref. 1, footnote 35.

izable, linear time-varying (Bayes matched) filter, followed by a zero-memory square-law device and a simple (or "ideal") integrator.†

The continuous form of $H(t_i,t_j) = h(t_i - t_j, t_i)$ [cf. Eq. (4.26)] follows directly from Eq. (4.11) and the preceding analysis if we observe that $G^{(2)}(t,u)$ may be identified with $\rho_c(t,u)_T$, which is (ψ times) the continuous version of $\rho_c(t_i,t_j)$ in Eqs. (4.27) and (4.28). The determining relation (4.28) is now

$$\rho_c(t,u)_T = \int_{0-}^{T+} h(x - t, x)h(x - u, x)\,dx \qquad 0- < t,\, u < T+$$
$$= 0 \qquad \text{elsewhere} \qquad (4.30)$$

The quadratic form Ψ_T [Eqs. (4.11)] becomes

$$\Psi_T(v) = \iint_{-\infty}^{\infty} V(t)\rho_c(t,u)_T V(u)\,dt\,du \qquad (4.31a)$$

$$= \int_{0-}^{T+} dt \left\{ \int_0^t V(\tau)h(t - \tau, t)\,d\tau \right\}^2 = \int_{0-}^{T+} V_F(t)^2\,dt \qquad (4.31b)$$

where $V_F(t)$ is given by the expression within the braces in Eq. (4.31b).

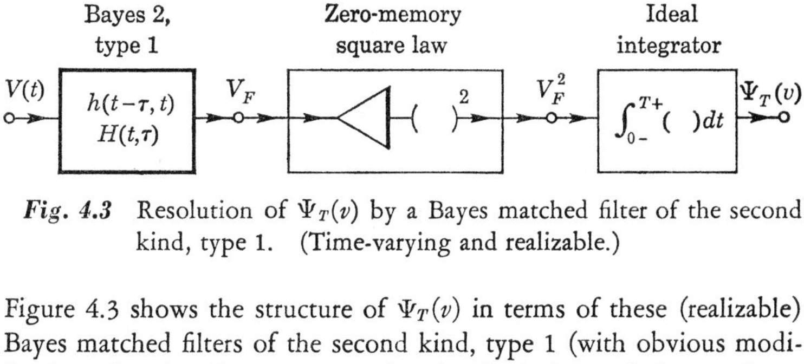

Fig. 4.3 Resolution of $\Psi_T(v)$ by a Bayes matched filter of the second kind, type 1. (Time-varying and realizable.)

Figure 4.3 shows the structure of $\Psi_T(v)$ in terms of these (realizable) Bayes matched filters of the second kind, type 1 (with obvious modifications for the discrete cases above). [Solutions of the nonlinear integral equation (4.30) for h are discussed in Ref. 1, p. 357.] Like the linear cases in Sec. 4.2, the quadratic form Ψ_n (or Ψ_T) may be resolved in a number of ways. A second, equivalent resolution of Eqs. (4.11)

† A more complex but alternative equivalent to this time-varying matched filter is (Bayes of the second kind) type 1*a*, consisting of an invariant realizable filter in conjunction with a time-varying switch; cf. Ref. 1, pp. 354–355. It is also possible to consider *nonrealizable* filters $\mathbf{Q}_0' = [H'(t_i,t_j)]$, which do not vanish ($t_j < t_i$), where again the basic relation is of the form (4.28) with h replaced by H' therein; cf. Ref. 1, p. 355. These may be classed as type 1*b*.

yields Bayes matched filters of the second kind, type 2. To see this, let us use Eq. (4.27) and observe that

$$[\rho_c(t_i,t_j)] \equiv [\hat{H}(t_i,t_j)] = [\hat{H}(t_j,t_i)] \tag{4.32}$$

represents a nonrealizable,† time-varying filter of weighting function $\rho_c \equiv \hat{H}$, etc. The constraints of nonrealizability can be removed, however, by the artifice of deleting all terms in ϱ_c below the diagonal and doubling those above it.‡ The result here is

$$\Psi_n = \sum_{ij}^{n} v_i v_j \hat{H}(t_i,t_j)\,\Delta t = \sum_{j=1}^{n} v_j \sum_{i=1}^{n} v_i \hat{h}(t_j - t_i, t_j)\,\Delta t \tag{4.33}$$

where $\hat{h}(t_j - t_i, t_j) = 2\epsilon_{ij}^{-1}\hat{H}(t_i,t_j)$, $t_j > t_i$, $= 0$, $t_j < t_i$, is now the weighting function of a realizable, time-varying linear filter, which is termed a

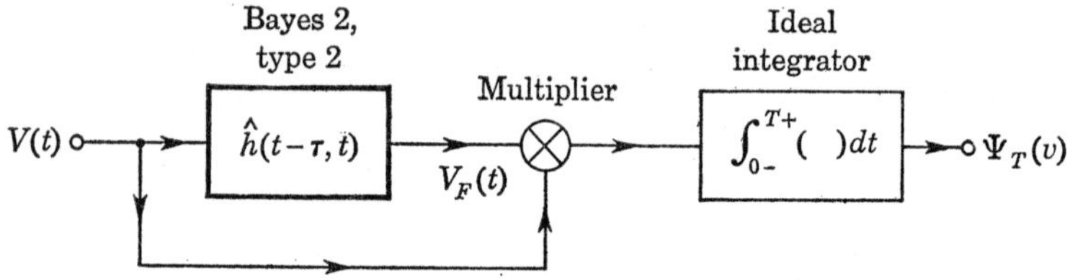

Fig. 4.4 Resolution of $\Psi_T(v)$ by a Bayes matched filter of the second kind, type 2. (Time-varying and realizable.)

Bayes matched filter of the second kind, type 2.§ Thus, we can write Eq. (4.33) as

$$\Psi_n = \sum_{j=1}^{n} v(t_j)\hat{v}_F(t_j)$$

with (4.34)

$$\hat{v}_F(t_j) \equiv \sum_{i=1}^{j} v(t_i)\hat{h}(t_j - t_i, t_j)\,\Delta t$$

so that the structure of Ψ_n is resolved into a sequence consisting of matched filter, ideal multiplier, and integrator (as shown in Fig. 4.4 for

† Because of the symmetry of ϱ_c.

‡ This follows for any symmetric quadratic form, for if $A_{ij} = A_{ji}$, we can write $\sum_{ij}^{n} A_{ij} = 2\sum_{j=1}^{n}\sum_{i=1}^{j} A_{ij}\epsilon_{ij}^{-1}$, $\epsilon_{ij} = 1$, $i \neq j$, and $\epsilon_{ij} = 2$, $i = j$, so that $\sum_{ij}^{n} A_{ij}$ is unchanged if we replace A_{ij} by 0; $i > j$.

§ The nonrealizable version, Eq. (4.32), is type 2*a*.

the continuous analogue). The continuous version of Eqs. (4.11) becomes now

$$\Psi_T(v) = \int_{0-}^{T+} \hat{V}_F(t)V(t)\,dt \tag{4.35}$$

with

$$\hat{V}_F(t) = \int_{0-}^{\infty\ (\text{or } t)} V(\tau)\hat{h}(t-\tau,\,t)\,d\tau \tag{4.35a}$$

where $\hat{h}(t-\tau,\,t) = 0$, $t < \tau$, for realizability. Unlike $h(t-\tau,\,t)$ of type 1 above, $\hat{h}$ is uniquely determined once ρ_c (or $\mathbf{C}^{(2)}$) is specified, since now $\hat{h}(t-\tau,\,t) = \rho_c(t,u)_T$ for $t > \tau$.

Under certain conditions still another class of matched filter for Ψ_n (or Ψ_T) is possible, closely related to, and identical in many cases with, the (S/N) matched filters of the earlier theory.[1] This class (Bayes matched filters of the second kind, type 3) arises whenever the symmetrical kernel $\mathbf{C}^{(2)}$ can be factored into the matrix product of two vectors, e.g., if

$$\mathbf{C}^{(2)} = \boldsymbol{\gamma}\tilde{\boldsymbol{\gamma}} = [\gamma_i\gamma_j] \tag{4.36}$$

where, as in Eq. (4.18), we may set

$$\boldsymbol{\gamma} \equiv [\hat{h}_M(T-t_i)\,\Delta t] \tag{4.37}$$

and $\hat{h}_M$ is now the weighting function of a time-invariant, realizable linear filter with readout at $t = T$, often achieved in practice with a suitable delay line and readout; here, of course, $\hat{h}_M \neq h_M$ [cf. Eq. (4.18)], since $\mathbf{C}^{(2)} \neq \mathbf{C}^{(1)}\mathbf{g}$ of Eqs. (4.10). Then, if Eq. (4.36) is true, we have at once

$$\Psi_n = (\tilde{\mathbf{v}}\boldsymbol{\gamma})(\tilde{\boldsymbol{\gamma}}\mathbf{v}) = (\tilde{\mathbf{v}}\boldsymbol{\gamma})^2 = \Big(\sum_{j=1}^{n} v(t_j)\hat{h}_M(T-t_j)\,\Delta t\Big)^2 \tag{4.38}$$

which is interpreted as the matched filter followed by ideal square-law rectification. Note that unlike the two cases preceding, there is *no* final integration. The continuous form of Eq. (4.38), with the help of the continuous version of Eq. (4.36), viz.,

$$G^{(2)}(t,u) = \hat{h}_M(T-t)\hat{h}_M(T-u) \qquad 0- < t,\, u < T+ \tag{4.39a}$$

becomes

$$\Psi_T(v) = \left(\int_{0-}^{T+} V(t)\hat{h}_M(T-t)\,dt\right)^2 \tag{4.39b}$$

Here $G^{(2)}$ vanishes outside $(0,T)$ because of the realizability of h_M and the readout at $t = T$.

This alternative resolution of $\Psi_T(v)$ is shown in Fig. 4.5. Once $\mathbf{C}^{(2)}$ [or $G^{(2)}$] is factored (whenever this can be done), $\hat{h}_M$ is determined directly from Eq. (4.37) or (4.39*a*), of course, and except for scale factors, $\hat{h}_M$ is unique.

Signals in additive normal noise again provide us with important examples. In these cases $\mathbf{C}^{(2)}$ ($\equiv \varrho_c\,\Delta t$) and $G^{(2)}(t,u)$ usually take the forms [cf. Eqs. (4.4*a*) and (4.5)]

$$\begin{aligned} \mathbf{C}^{(2)} &= \psi^{-2}\mathbf{k}_N^{-1}\mathbf{k}_S\mathbf{k}_N^{-1} \\ G^{(2)}(t,u) &= \rho_c(t,u)_T = \psi\langle D_T(t,u)\rangle \end{aligned} \qquad (4.40)$$

where $\langle D_T(t,u)\rangle$ is given by Eq. (2.58*c*) for narrow-band signals, or by

$$\begin{aligned} \langle D_T(t,u)\rangle &\equiv \langle X_T(t;\boldsymbol{\theta})X_T(u;\boldsymbol{\theta})\rangle_\theta & 0;<t,\ u<T+ \\ &= 0 & \text{elsewhere} \end{aligned} \qquad (4.41)$$

for general signals.† With continuous sampling the type 1 Bayes filter

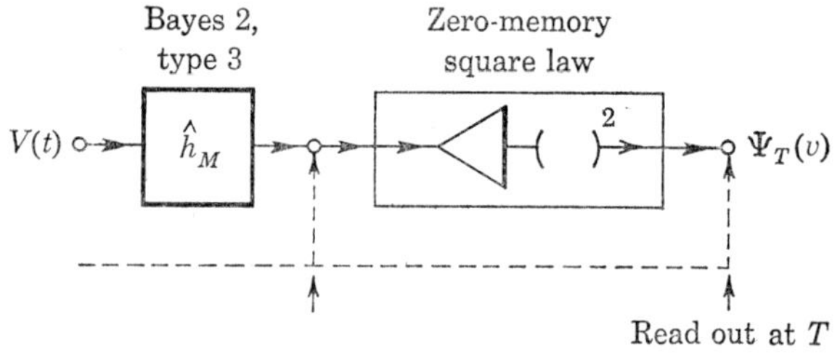

Fig. 4.5 Resolution of $\Psi_T(v)$ by a Bayes matched filter of the second kind, type 3. (Invariant and realizable.)

of the second kind may be represented by a product of time-varying gains $g_m(t)$ and realizable, invariant delay-line filters‡ h_m:

$$h(t-u,\ t) = \sum_{m=0}^{\infty} g_m(t)h_m(T-x) \qquad \text{with } h_m = \epsilon_m \cos 2\pi m(T-x) \qquad (4.42)$$

where the h_m vanish for $x > T$ and the $g_m(t)[= g_{-m}(t)]$ vanish outside

† Eq. (A.16) and Ref. 2, sec. 20.2-2, especially pp. 854–856. Note again that ρ_c here equals $\psi\rho_G$; cf. eq. (20.52) in Ref. 2.

‡ As long as $\rho_c(t,u)_T$ is continuous, as well as positive-definite and symmetrical; cf. Ref. 1, sec. C.

the interval $(0-,T+)$. The time-varying gains $g_m(t)$ are equal to $\lambda_m\varphi_m(t) \cdot T^{-1/2}$, where the λ_m and φ_m are the eigenvalues and eigenfunctions of the homogeneous integral equation;† i.e.,

$$\int_0^T \rho_c(t,u)_T\, \varphi_m(u)\, du = \lambda_m\varphi_m(t) \qquad 0 \le t \le T \tag{4.43}$$

Similarly, $\hat{h}$ for the matched filter of type 2, second kind [cf. Eq. (4.35*a*)] is given by $\rho_c(t,u)_T$ when $t > u$, while $\hat{h}_M$, [type 3, second kind, Eqs. (4.37) to (4.39)] is only possible when $\mathbf{C}^{(2)}$, or $\langle D_T(t,u)\rangle$ [Eq. (4.41)], factors. With white noise backgrounds one has‡

$$\langle D_T(t,u)\rangle = \frac{4}{W_0^2}\langle s(t;\boldsymbol{\theta})s(u;\boldsymbol{\theta})\rangle \tag{4.44a}$$

or

$$\langle D_T(t,u)\rangle = \frac{4}{W_0^2}\langle F_s(t;\boldsymbol{\theta}_0)F_s(u;\boldsymbol{\theta}_0)\cos[\omega_0(t-u) - \varphi_s(t;\boldsymbol{\theta}_0) + \varphi_s(u;\boldsymbol{\theta})]\rangle \tag{4.44b}$$

respectively for general and narrow-band signals, so that from Eqs. (4.11) we may write

$$a_0^2\Psi_T\Big|_{\text{white}} = \frac{2A_0^2}{W_0^2}\iint_0^T V(t)\langle s(t;\boldsymbol{\theta})s(u;\boldsymbol{\theta})\rangle V(u)\, dt\, du \tag{4.45}$$

or, equivalently, with Eq. (4.46*b*) in place of (4.44*a*) in Eq. (4.45) for the narrow-band cases.

4.4 *Remarks*

In Secs. 4.2 and 4.3 we have shown how the earlier concepts[5,6] of the matched filter may be generalized by explicitly taking into account the element of decision making which is inherent in signal detection and extraction. The earlier, so-called "S/N" matched filters are accordingly replaced by Bayes matched filters, defined as linear operations on the received waveforms $V(t)$ when a Bayes criterion for detection or extraction is chosen. For the important cases where the Bayes system may be expressed as a function of quadratic forms in the received data [cf. Sec. 4.1 and Eqs. (4.10) and (4.11)] we have distinguished two

† With white noise backgrounds any complete orthonormal set $\{\varphi_m\}$ may be used.
‡ Ref. 2, sec. 20.2-3, especially eqs. (20.66*a*) and (20.67*f*).

principal classes of matched filter, with a variety of types within these classes. Table 4.1 summarizes their main features.

In some cases Bayes matched filters have the same structure as the S/N matched filter, e.g., Bayes type 1, first kind, and type 3, second kind. As we have noted above, the latter occur when $\langle D_T(t,u) \rangle$ [Eqs. (4.41) and (4.44)] factors, which is only possible when $X_T(t;\boldsymbol{\theta})$ [or $s(t;\boldsymbol{\theta})$ in the white-noise situation] is independent of the (random) parameters† $\boldsymbol{\theta}$. However, when a structural identity between the Bayes and S/N matched filters does occur, we observe that this is *not* an inherent property of the matched-filter concept as such. It is, instead, the result of (1) the particular signal and noise statistics involved and (2) the fact that in both instances the respective optimizations are based on identical quadratic forms, involving the effective signal and noise energies, so that enhancement of signal vis-à-vis the noise in each case leads to the same matched filters, although for quite different criteria. Since the Bayes matched filters are the result of an actual decision process, minimizing average cost or risk, where all pertinent knowledge (and ignorance) has been systematically used in achieving optimality, whereas the S/N formulation is based on the more limited and less complete criterion of signal-to-noise ratio, the Bayes matched filter is the broader and more fundamental concept. This concept subsumes that of the S/N matched filter, just as second-moment operations (e.g., spectra, covariance functions) are subsumed by the statistically more complete operations based on the nth-order distributions of the signal and noise processes involved in detection and extraction. For these reasons, also, the structure of Bayes matched filters may differ considerably from those based on the more elementary criterion. The latter, while useful, may depart significantly from the optimum. This must be weighted against their frequently greater simplicity and economy, and the important feature that they depend only on the covariances of the noise (and signal) processes, and not on the higher-order statistics required in the Bayes theory. Finally, we remark that Bayes matched filters of the second kind are not restricted to deterministic signals: the analysis of Sec. 4.3 applies also when the desired signals, as well as the background noise, are entirely stochastic.

† For example, in coherent detection and extraction, when only the signal amplitude may be regarded as random at the receiver, or for incoherent detection and extraction of *narrow-band* signals, where, in addition to amplitude, only the RF phase (or epoch) is random; Ref. 2, p. 864 and prob. 20.6 on p. 869.

Table 4.1 Bayes Matched Filters

Elements of Bayes system	Class and type	Structure	Comments
$\Phi_T(v) = \psi \int\int v(t) G^{(1)}(t,u) g(u)\, dt\, du$ ($\Phi_n = \tilde{\mathbf{v}} \mathbf{C}^{(1)} \mathbf{g}$ [Eqs. (4.10)])	1st kind type 1	$h_M(T - t)$ [Fig. 4.1]	Invariant, realizable, unique $\equiv S/N$ matched filter [cf. Eqs. (4.18), (4.20)].
	1st kind type 2	$H_c(t,u) = h_c(t - u, t)$ [Fig. 4.2]	Time-varying, nonrealizable, unique [Eqs. (4.15), (4.21)].
$\psi_T(v) = \psi \int\int v(t) G^{(2)}(t,u) v(u)\, dt\, du$ $\psi_n = \tilde{\mathbf{v}} \mathbf{C}^{(2)} \mathbf{v}$ [Eqs. (4.11)]	2d kind type 1	$h(t - u,t)$ [Fig. 4.3]	Time-varying, realizable, not unique [Eqs. (4.30), (4.42)].
	2d kind type 2	$\hat{h}(t - u,t) = \rho_c(t,u)_T \; (t > u)$ [Fig. 4.4]	Time-varying, realizable, unique [Eqs. (4.31*a*); (4.32)–(4.35)].
	2d kind type 3	$\hat{h}_M(T - t)$ [Fig. 4.5]	Invariant, realizable, unique $\equiv S/N$ matched filter; not possible unless $\mathbf{C}^{(2)}$, or ρ_c, factors [Eq. (4.37)].

References

1. Middleton, D.: On New Classes of Matched Filters and Generalizations of the Matched Filter Concept, *IRE, Trans. Inform. Theory*, **IT-6**:349 (1960).
2. ———: "An Introduction to Statistical Communication Theory," McGraw-Hill Book Company, New York, 1960.
3. ———: Optimization Problems in Statistical Communication Theory, in R. Bellman (ed.): "Mathematical Optimization Techniques," chap. 7, University of California Press, Berkeley, Calif., 1963.
4. ———: Canonically Optimum Threshold Detection, *RAND Memorandum*. (In preparation.)
5. Van Vleck, J. H., and D. Middleton: A Theoretical Comparison of the Visual, Aural, and Meter Reception of Pulsed Signals in the Presence of Noise, *J. Appl. Phys.*, **17**:940 (1946).
6. North, D. O.: Analysis of the Factors Which Determine Signal-to-Noise Discrimination in Radar, *RCA Lab. Tech. Rept.* PTR-6C, Princeton, N.J., June, 1943; also *Proc. IEEE*, **51**:1016 (1963).
7. Wainstein, L. A., and V. D. Zubakov: "Extraction of Signals from Noise," trans. by R. A. Silverman, Prentice-Hall, Inc., Englewood Cliffs, N.J., 1962.

Chapter 5 Critique, Extensions, and Future Problems

In the preceding chapters we have presented a formal development of decision-theory methods for a variety of fundamental problems in communication theory (Chap. 1). These include signal detection (Chap. 2), signal extraction (Chap. 3), and the realizations of optimum system structures for such purposes (Chap. 4). The general results have been illustrated with several simple but important examples where for the most part a rather complete analytical treatment is possible. Such completeness can be deceptive, however: as in all attempts to model "reality," simplification, approximation, and compromise are more the rule than the exception, if we are to reach quantitative goals. The constant effort is to broaden concept and to increase the effectiveness of method, while still maintaining tractable procedures. For these reasons it is necessary to distinguish between the real advantages and difficulties of decision-theory techniques here, and to indicate how the former can be exploited and the latter overcome or mitigated. Accordingly, we begin with a short critique, below, of the general approach[1]

(Sec. 5.1). For further consideration we also mention some of the recent studies that are representative of the kinds of generalizations and extensions to be expected in the applications of these methods in many areas (Sec. 5.2). Section 5.3 concludes our discussion with comments on future problems and developments.

5.1 *Critique*†

Let us begin with some of the achievements of the decision-theory approach in communication theory. First, we observe that the method is quite general, not only in the way that it uses all available information, but also in the ways that it provides of incorporating the observer's "ignorance," as well—exhibited, for example, in the nonzero or non-unity values of the a priori signal probabilities or in the random character of signal parameters. The approach also provides us with the three chief elements of an effective theory: (1) a representation of optimum system structure, (2) evaluation of the expected performance of this optimum system, and (3) a quantitative method for the consistent comparison of actual suboptimum systems with the theoretical optimum. As we have indicated in Chaps. 2 to 4, an explicit theory is possible, giving us elements (1) to (3) in detail.

Apart from specific systems and their evaluation, decision-theory methods also offer us a much broader and potentially more realistic technique of system design than do earlier methods based on lower-order statistics, e.g., the spectra, correlation functions, and second-order distribution densities, characteristic of analyses based on calculations of signal-to-noise ratio, for instance. These latter, though useful because they are readily calculable, are incomplete, not only statistically, but also in formulation; the essential decision features of detection or estimation are omitted, and the full implications of the underlying assumptions are not always evident. With a decision-theory formulation, on the other hand, the assumptions and constraints of any particular problem are brought out into the open by its very formulation as a statistical decision process. The analyst and system designer is forced at the outset to a careful statement of the problem. After this, the various results, (1) to (3) above, follow according to the indicated operations and the available a priori information.

Theory also provides a definite method for handling new situations, where current experience and intuition may be inadequate. A systematic approach to system design is another important feature which

† The material of this section is based principally on Ref. 1, sec. 23.4.

permits us not only to obtain the explicit operations on the data but to interpret these operations as ordered sequences of realizable physical elements, available to the practicing engineer (Chap. 4). Perhaps the least exploited feature is the comparison of systems. We remark in this connection that actual systems are never strictly equivalent to the corresponding optima derived from theory. However, the theoretical optimum not only provides a limit on expected performance which the actual systems can approach but also acts as a guide to the designer. The real, approximate system should embody the significant features of the optimum structure. Similarly, suboptimum systems can be compared, not only with the optimum, but with one another. We should not, however, gain the impression that decision-theory methods are without limitations or that they can always be applied for equally effective results. The very generality of the approach puts demands on the model which are never met fully, and sometimes met only slightly, in practice. There are three main areas where a decision-theory model presents difficulties: (1) in the apparent arbitrariness of the cost assignments, (2) in the inadequacy of the a priori information, and (3) sometimes in the selection of the criterion of optimality itself.

Let us begin with (1). We observe first that it is not possible to assign costs accurately from an objective viewpoint. As soon as we attempt this, subjective elements creep in, and we are forced to admit that our particular problem does not possess unique costs of decision. Actually, this lack of objectivity (or uniqueness) in cost is not a difficulty inherent in our communication applications alone but is basic to all areas where we wish in some sense to match a model to the real world. The subjectivity of the cost assignments here simply reflects the *unavoidable uncertainty* regarding costs that is the price we must pay for an inevitably incomplete knowledge of the world around us, and *as such should be accepted as part of the model.* In fact, from this viewpoint, the lack of uniqueness is not a defect but is rather a mark of realism.

Moreover, an important mitigating feature here is the invariance of optimum system structure in detection with respect to cost assignments [as embodied in the threshold $\mathcal{K}$; cf. Eq. (2.25)]: no matter what costs are selected for the possible outcomes, the mode of processing the data remains unchanged. This invariance is, of course, usually vital in most practical situations. It would be almost always prohibitively expensive to have to redesign the system for each new cost assignment. Similar statements can be made about extraction systems, although now many more classes of optimal systems are possible, depending on the choice of cost function.† Often, we ourselves make the cost selection which in our best judgment at the time is most suitable, recognizing that this is precisely what we in effect do in all decision situations.

The question of inadequacy of the a priori information may be considered as similar to our inability to fix costs uniquely for a given situation. Here we regard a priori information (embodied as the *functional form* of probability distributions, the known signal parameters, specific noise spectra, and the like) as a measure of our subjective awareness of the facts of the detection or extraction situation in question.[2] Similarly, lack of a priori data (which may appear as a signal parameter regarded as a random variable, or as an unknown probability or d.d., etc.) is our subjective awareness of ignorance in respect to these quantities. Just as cost assignment is ultimately subjective, so also is the assignment of probabilities, probability densities, and the like, to our model a subjective judgment, helped along with whatever facts we may possess from previous experience.

Lack of a priori information can be overcome in a number of more or less satisfactory ways. One approach, almost impossible to achieve in practice, is to acquire all the needed data and then build and operate the system accordingly. A more realistic approach applies some additional extremal principle, subject perhaps to one or more constraints: Minimax, maximum likelihood, and so on. A disadvantage is that usually different extremal principles lead to different results. Frequently, circumstances (i.e., the environment in which our particular decision process is embedded) will narrow down the choice of possibilities and sometimes, in special instances, eliminate all but one. In any case, the more uncertain the a priori data, the greater the expected cost of operation—we cannot avoid paying for ignorance. It should be pointed out, however, that lack of a priori data makes the design of a Bayes system difficult. Moreover, the additional extremal principles invoked to remedy this shortage can have their own drawbacks, which limit the scope of their applicability; Minimax tends to be too conservative, for example.

The choice of criterion itself is arbitrary. Here our selection is always a compromise between realism and mathematical simplicity: we

† In fact, we observe that $\mathbf{T}_{R\text{-opt}}^{(N)}$, whether it be for detection or extraction, is some function of the a priori d.d. F_n [cf. Eq. (2.23)] or its logarithm. Thus, optimum structure (and performance) depend directly on F_n; in this way detection and extraction are closely related conceptually, while they can be quite "distant" in detailed structure (cf. beginning of Chap. 4).

attempt to construct a criterion which fits a broad class of situations and at the same time permits us to reach some definite numerical conclusions. The notion of cost, or risk, is a natural and general quantitative interpretation of more subtle value judgments, an interpretation which, as employed in its present form, also yields quantitative results. Minimization of average cost, or risk, is, of course, just one possible criterion of performance (cf. Sec. 1.3). Other more elaborate ones can be constructed: minimization of the cost variance, subject to fixed average risk, for example, might be more appropriate in some situations. The point is that different criteria lead to different results, so that again it is our subjective choice, now of criteria, which inescapably influences our decisions and the way in which they are arrived at.

Finally, a practical limitation on the utility of decision-theoretic methods is analytical complexity. Overall optimization of many-link systems in this fashion so far appears to be intractable, so that other techniques must be employed, such as dynamic programming,[3,4] which, however, may profitably use the results of the decision-theory approach to provide the details of individual link performance needed in the analysis of the overall system. As we have remarked earlier, the important threshold cases can be handled, while a corresponding treatment for strong signals is often intractable. However, a system designed for optimum or near-optimum performance at threshold signal levels will usually be quite satisfactory at the higher ones.

Let us summarize the preceding comments. The decision-theoretic approach provides a unified, quantitative theory of system optimality, design, evaluation, and comparison. These methods, however, are limited and qualified by the observer's judgment, the available a priori information, and the degree of realism (and hence analytical complexity) he wishes to incorporate into his models. The search for optimality should not be pushed too far; the principal role of an optimum system (which can never be strictly realized in practice) is to provide a limiting measure of performance and a guide to system structure for the approximations actually used in applications. Optimality is also qualified by its lack of uniqueness in general: different criteria lead to different results.

In the discussion of optimality we should not overlook the significance of different degrees of improvement that may be achieved over corresponding suboptimum systems. Some such systems may be "close to," and others "far from," the theoretical limiting performance. Just what this means depends, of course, on the larger question of the system's role in the communication environment. For example, a difference of a few decibels in certain situations may be quite ignorable or not worth the great increase in structural complexity needed for essentially optimum performance. On the other hand, a few decibels can also mean a significant improvement in overall performance. This is particularly true in systems where low error rates are required, with a consequent high rate of decision. For example, an increase or decrease of a few decibels in the input signal-to-noise (power) ratio can produce a corresponding increase or decrease of several orders of magnitude in the error probabilities of decision, which may in turn become quite significant for conditions involving high decision rates. The reason for this large shift in the magnitude of the error probabilities is the initial requirement of very small error probabilities per decision; in effect, we are operating well out on the "tail" of the curve for the d.d. in question, so that comparatively small changes in the variance (as measured by changes in the signal-to-noise ratio) produce large changes in the type 1 and 2 error probabilities. A few decibels may also represent a significant change, even when a high decision rate is not required. For example, in radar 3 db can imply an expansion or contraction of effective threshold range by as much as 40 per cent.

So far we have considered some of the achievements and difficulties of the decision-theory approach. It is also instructive to consider the extent by which decision- and information-theory methods[5–7] both differ and overlap. Here "information theory" is defined in the strict sense, as a theory of information measures and coding.† The difference between the two is partly a matter of emphasis. Thus, in information theory it is the maximization of average rate of message transmission by suitable encoding, subject to the constraints of the channel (i.e., the noise and the fidelity requirements at the receiver) that is the principal aim. The significance of the message set and the outcomes of particular transmissions are of secondary importance. On the other hand, in applications of decision theory to communication problems it is precisely these latter factors which are of chief concern; here the reception process (and the transmission process, also, through proper selection of signal‡) is governed by the value judgments associated with the possible decisions which represent the final output from the communication link.

† Ref. 1, sec. 6.1.
‡ Ref. 1, sec. 23.2.

The former (i.e., informational) approach is naturally suited to the many situations where one wishes to minimize the cost of utilizing the channel, as in commercial telephone operation, for example. The latter (or decision-theory method) arises where channel considerations are secondary (except, of course, as they influence the physics of the communication process itself). This is the case where the significance of particular messages and the decisions consequent upon them are of principal concern. For example, in radar we normally seek to minimize the cost of decision error, not necessarily to maximize the rate of information transmission. These two viewpoints frequently lead to different results. The reason is that each criterion emphasizes different aspects of performance—the magnitude of average risk is improved by lowering the probabilities of decision errors (for fixed costs), whereas the criterion of information loss favors a system in which the *posterior* signal probabilities before and after the system operation are nearly equal. A small error rate is not necessarily accompanied by a small information loss.

When the role of the finite sample is specifically taken into account, i.e., when the error probabilities in reception are necessarily nonvanishing, the information- and decision-theory approaches may overlap to varying extents in both method and viewpoint. The recovery and reception of encoded messages are not now simply a matter of applying the inverse operation to the encoding process, e.g., of setting $\boldsymbol{T}_{\mathrm{R}} = \boldsymbol{T}_{\mathrm{T}}^{-1}$. Reception is no longer directly related to transmission but requires separate attention and adjustment. As noted earlier, finite error probabilities in reception imply a decision process, and it is precisely here that the techniques of decision theory are applied. Finally, we observe that the information- and decision-theory approaches are also connected through the selection of cost functions: in place of the usual constant cost or difference cost assignments of detection and estimation, we can use a cost function based on a measure of uncertainty, or on an equivocation when we are concerned with information rate.† In this way the two approaches, though different in scope and emphasis, complement each other in the attack on the basic problems of system optimization, design, and evaluation.

5.2 *Extensions*

Much has already been accomplished in the effort to generalize and extend earlier models and applications and to overcome the difficulties

† Ref. 1, chap. 22.

cited in the previous section.† The introduction of greater mathematical rigor and more powerful analytical tools has also accompanied an expanding realism in three principal areas of the communication process: (1) the modeling of the medium, (2) the nature and mechanism of coupling to the medium, and (3) the processing of the transmitted and received data. The first requires an appropriate interpretation of the physics of the medium and propagation in and through it. The aim here is to obtain the space-time operations that represent medium and source interaction. The second involves the various arrays, apertures, and "transducers," by which these space-time phenomena are sensed in reception and introduced into the medium on transmission. The third, of course, embodies the operations that are required to project or extract the desired information in this general communication system. All three elements are contained in our operator formalism

$$\{v\} = \boldsymbol{T}_R^{(N)} \boldsymbol{T}_M^{(N)} \boldsymbol{T}_T^{(N)} \{u\} \tag{5.1}$$

discussed as Eq. (1.1) earlier. By suitably modifying the adjustable components of these operators we can obtain different degrees of optimality, as we have already seen in the preceding chapters.

In the light of current efforts let us consider the medium, coupling, and processing in a little more detail. Model building, or modeling the medium, i.e., determining $\boldsymbol{T}_M^{(N)}$, is critical to the success of any effective communication operation. Earlier models were usually deterministic and stationary. Spatial effects did not appear explicitly, and the resulting operators were functions of time alone. For many purposes this has been sufficient, but as the areas of application have broadened, greater sophistication has become necessary: time-varying media with both random and deterministic components have been introduced, characteristic of scatter-multipath conditions, for example, in radio, radar, radio astronomy, and underwater sound propagation.[8–11] Thus, for example, we may seek representations of the medium's behavior in terms of a suitable response or weighting function

$$h_M(t,\tau) = h(t,\tau)_D + h(t,\tau)_R \tag{5.2}$$

where h_D, h_R are the possible deterministic and random components, the former accounting for discrete multipath phenomena and the latter

† See, for example, Ref. 1, chaps. 19–23, and, for many developments since 1960, Ref. 17.

for the random, multiplicative effects introduced by inhomogeneities, etc.

Moreover, we now have to deal with stochastic space-time fields, where the phenomena in question are random not only in time but over space, as well. Here only discrete sampling (in space) is possible for the many purposes where we have to reconstruct such fields, predict their behavior, and study them experimentally.[12,13] Complex signal sources, scattering mechanisms, inhomogeneities, and distributed targets are typical of the problems treated in the drive toward greater realism in constructing $T_M^{(N)}$, and consequently greater realism and effectiveness in system design and optimization.

The data that are processed in the receiver are strongly influenced by the sensors that provide the actual, physical coupling of the receiver to the medium. Since the size and distribution of the coupling elements determine, among other things, the strength of the received signals, the spatial orientation of these elements is likewise an important factor modifying the received data. In this fashion the spatial as well as the temporal character of the data field must be taken into consideration: the coupling, or "transducers," act as mapping operations that convert the space-time data into time-dependent processes for subsequent handling in the receiver. The arrays whereby such mapping operations are accomplished can often be adjusted for further optimization of overall performance. Subsequent processing, of course, depends on array structure in an intricate way. Sometimes, also, it is possible to adjust and optimize array configurations without altering the specific structure of this subsequent processing, with the advantage that different arrays can be used without a change in the (usually involved) processing itself.[14] Similar remarks apply at the transmitting end ($\sim T_T$) of our system. In any case, the distributed nature of these arrays, as well as the distributed nature of sources and targets, are now to varying degrees being taken into account, in a more realistic program of system design and evaluation.

Advanced applications of the methods outlined in Chap. 1 have also been made in the "signal-processing" area. A few examples suffice to indicate the character of current efforts. For instance, the simple binary theory of detection (Chap. 2) has been extended to multiple alternative cases, in a variety of important radar and communications situations, including space communications.[†,15,16] The cost-coding,

† Ref. 1, sec. 23.1. (See also Ref. 17, p. 261.)

or signal-design, problem has received considerable attention,[15–17] as has the theory of *ambiguity functions* in this connection.[17] The effects of nonnormal noise on system performance have also been studied in the case of simple correlation detectors,[18] while multipath and scatter communication in noisy environments have been rather extensively examined.[9–11] Nor has attention been confined to detection only: much has also been done on signal estimation; we note, for example, the estimation of target range and velocity in radar,[19] in addition to target cross section (Sec. 3.4), and the estimation and extraction of signal waveform in communication applications.

In the case of stochastic signals interesting analytical questions arise when we attempt to construct applicable mathematical models. For gaussian signals in additive normal noise backgrounds various forms of necessary and sufficient (n. + s.) conditions for singularity† and nonsingularity have been established.[20–22,24] For normal processes with rational spectra the conditions take the simple form

$$\begin{aligned} \lim_{f\to\infty} \mathcal{W}_2(f)/\mathcal{W}_1(f) &\neq 1 \qquad \text{n. + s. condition for } \textit{singularity} \\ &= 1 \qquad \text{n. + s. condition for } \textit{nonsingularity} \end{aligned} \tag{5.3}$$

where $\mathcal{W}_{1,2}(f)$ are the respective power spectral densities of the two processes. An (additive) white noise background is a sufficient condition here for nonsingularity, so that our usual models are appropriate to the physical situations we wish to describe. Similarly, for deterministic signals a sufficient condition [on any interval $(0,T)$] is[23]

$$\int_{-\infty}^{\infty} \frac{|S(f)|^2}{\mathcal{W}_N(f)}\, df < \infty \tag{5.4}$$

where $S(f)$ is the amplitude spectrum of the sure signal and $\mathcal{W}_N(f)$ is the intensity spectrum of the accompanying normal noise. The theory for random signals, however, is more difficult and not yet as fully developed as in the case of deterministic signals. This reflects the more serious technical problems that are encountered in what, statistically, are essentially tests for variances in the former instances, as opposed to what are essentially tests for means in the latter cases.‡

† *Perfect* detection and extraction on an arbitrary interval (singularity), versus operation with nonzero probabilities of error (nonsingularity).

‡ A discussion of the applicability of the analysis to practical situations is given in Ref. 20, sec. 7; Ref. 21; and Ref. 23, sec. 4. See also Ref. 17, p. 232, for further references.

Other active areas involve the study of criteria and comparison of systems,[25] matched and inverse filters (cf. Chap. 4), sequential detection,[26] pattern recognition,[27] and coding, which is a field in itself.† Adaptive systems and systems designed to be distribution-free or otherwise to operate independently of statistical parameters have been developed in special cases.‡ Adaptive control,[28,29] artificial intelligence, human information processing, and machine "learning" are also contiguous domains where the fundamental methods of a generalized communication theory have fruitful applications. The References and Bibliography at the end of this chapter and, in particular, a careful study of Ref. 17 will provide the reader with a much more detailed and complete picture of recent activities.

5.3 *Future Problems*

From the foregoing it is clear that the basic methods of a statistical communication theory have already penetrated into almost all areas where random phenomena occur and where processing and decision making in the face of uncertainty are required. The list of these areas is impressive:

1. Electronics, including terrestrial and space communications
2. Radar and radio astronomy
3. Optics
4. Underwater sound
5. Meteorology (weather prediction)
6. Seismology
7. Electromechanics (servo and control)
8. Mechanics (structures under random forces)
9. Aerodynamics (in addition to area 5)

to mention the principal ones. In all cases above we are concerned with signal propagation, detection, and extraction in media of varying complexity, under a wide range of operating conditions, and a multitude of applications ranging from an exploration of the physical and statistical properties of the medium to the detection (and classification of) targets, signal sources, and the transmission of information generally. The first group (cases 1–3) are primarily electromagnetic phenomena, while the second and third, (cases 4–9) are basically mechanical; all are,

† See the Bibliography that follows this chapter.
‡ See, for example, Ref. 17, and references therein.

for applied purposes, dominated by a variety of statistical phenomena, or "noise," which macroscopically limits the precision of observation and processing.

Because of the simpler nature of the media and the statistical mechanisms in cases 1 and 2 above, these areas are currently further developed than are the others vis-à-vis the application of communication theory methods. The advent of the laser (coherent light source) and the general improvement in the physical scope and capabilities of system components, however, are bringing case 3 and most of the others (cases 4 to 9) to a similar level of development.

What, then, are some of the present needs and expected future developments? To begin with, it is evident that the need for greater realism in our analytical models of media and systems is still with us in most instances; what is often adequate for the present (because we cannot do better at the moment) is no longer enough for the demands of the future. In all cases we must now recognize and deal explicitly with the essential SPACE-TIME features of the phenomena in question (*vide* especially p. 101).

One area of particular importance which is still, from the viewpoint of signal detection and extraction, in its quantitative infancy is the theory of adaptive systems. Such questions as what to adapt to and how much is gained by adaptation and the more difficult ones of *how* to carry out the adaptive operation, the conditions for its convergence, and its rate of convergence all require attention. Another area of increasing importance is the experimental study of the properties of the media, particularly in underwater sound, optics, meteorology, and seismology. Here signal processing techniques provide the essential tools for investigation and model building. Signal design (cost coding) is also required for effective interrogation of the medium. Further development of canonical structures is likewise needed, to help diminish our dependence on what is often too high an order of statistical knowledge and to indicate systems that are relatively insensitive to fluctuations in the statistical character of the random processes and fields involved. Such systems, of course, are generally not as effective as those designed to operate (optimally) under greater a priori information, but their desired advantage is often their invariance to our ignorance of a priori data. We may expect, accordingly, a continuing growth of such distribution-free and nonparametric approaches.

We may expect, also, a great increase in the use of computers for optimal signal detection and estimation. Computers can be programmed to adapt to, or "learn" in, an environment, and they are particularly suited to solving differential equations with boundary conditions. Thus, for example, we may first cast the usual integral equation formulations that optimum detection and extraction theory provide into the corresponding differential equations with constraints (e.g., boundary conditions). Then we may next employ computers to obtain from the received data the equivalents of the likelihood ratio and its functions (for extraction), under both soft (i.e., integral, etc.) and hard (i.e., maximum value) constraints. For the latter, Pontryagin's maximum principle is particularly suited.† In this way we may also expect other well-established methods of control theory, in turn, to provide important additional tools for signal processing. Results here, of course, are quasi-analytical in that specific solutions are found for specific input data; an optimization *procedure* is provided, but a set of computations must be carried out in each instance. Thus, optimal system design here takes the form of a computer with certain general capabilities and a set of programs, constructed to provide the needed adaptive functions, in contrast to the cases where analytical solutions for the ensemble of possible inputs and models can be obtained. Both are important and complementary approaches which will see extensive further development.

Formulation of desiderata is a first step toward their fulfillment, and from this, in turn, come many of the important problems of the future in communication theory, which we can summarize in a general way from our discussion above. In brief, we may expect important developments: in model building, particularly for time-varying random media that are both linear[31] and nonlinear; in the theory and practice of adaptive systems; in the treatment of *stochastic fields* for reconstruction,[32] detection, and extraction; in nonparametric systems; signal optimization (cost coding); canonical results which bring large numbers of special results into a common formalism and general method of treatment; new physical elements and components that will make possible cheaper and more effective realization of systems; general computers for optimal system performance, including new coding techniques; and, paralleling all this, a commensurate development of our understanding of the human being's role as a "communication system" in processing and decision making.

† For applications in signal design theory, see Ref. 30.

References

1. Middleton, D.: "An Introduction to Statistical Communication Theory," McGraw-Hill Book Company, New York, 1960.
2. Savage, L. J.: "The Foundations of Statistics," John Wiley & Sons, Inc., New York, 1954.
3. Bellman, R., and R. E. Kalaba: On the Role of Dynamic Programming in Statistical Communication Theory, *IRE, Trans. Inform. Theory,* **IT-3**:197 (1957).
4. Bellman, R.: "Dynamic Programming," Princeton University Press, Princeton, N.J., 1957.
5. Shannon, C. E.: A Mathematical Theory of Communication, *Bell System Tech. J.*, **27**:379, 623 (1948).
6. Fano, R. M.: "Transmission of Information," The Technology Press of the Massachusetts Institute of Technology, Cambridge, Mass., and John Wiley & Sons, Inc., New York, 1961.
7. Reza, F. M.: "An Introduction to Information Theory," McGraw-Hill Book Company, New York, 1961.
8. Turin, G.: Error Probabilities for Binary Symmetric Ideal Reception through Nonselective Slow Fading and Noise, *Proc. IRE*, **46**:1603–1619 (1958).
9. Price, R., and P. E. Green, Jr.: A Communication Technique for Multipath Channels, *Proc. IRE*, **46**:550–570 (1958).
10. Kailath, T.: "Adaptive Matched Filters," chap. 6, and references therein; cf. R. Bellman (ed.), "Mathematical Optimization Techniques," University of California Press, Berkeley, Calif., 1963.
11. Price, R.: "Binary Signaling over Very Noisy Incoherent Channels," Lincoln Laboratory Publications, McGraw-Hill Book Company, New York. (In preparation.)
12. Petersen, D. P., and D. Middleton: Sampling and Reconstruction of Wave-number-limited Functions in N-dimensional Euclidean Spaces, *Inform. Control*, **5**:279 (1962).
13. ——— and ———: On Representative Observations, *Tellus*, **15**(4):87 (1963). See also D. P. Petersen: "Sampling of Space-Time Stochastic Processes with Applications to Information and Decision Systems, D.E.S. dissertation, Rensselaer Polytechnic Institute, Troy, N.Y., 1963.
14. Middleton, D., and H. L. Groginsky: Detection of Random Acoustic Signals by Receivers with Distributed Elements: Optimum Receiver Structures for Normal Noise and Signal Fields, *Raytheon Co. Submarine Signal Div. Rept.* R 297, August, 1963; also, submitted to *JASA* (1964).
15. Nuttall, A. H.: Error Probabilities for Equi-correlated M-ary Signals under Phase-coherent and Phase-incoherent Reception, *IRE, Trans. Inform. Theory*, **IT-8**:305 (1962). (See also the extensive bibliography therein.)
16. Balakrishnan, A. V.: A Contribution to the Sphere-packing Problem of Communication Theory, *J. Math. Anal. Appl.*, **3**:485, 1961.

17. Zadeh, L. A., (ed.): Report on Progress in Information Theory in the U.S.A., 1960–1963, *IEEE, Trans. Inform. Theory*, **IT-9**:221–264 (1963). (See p. 241.)
18. Middleton, D.: Acoustic Signal Detection by Simple Correlators in the Presence of Non-gaussian Noise: I. Signal-to-Noise Ratios and Canonical Forms, *JASA*, **34**:1598–1609 (1962); II. Error Probabilities and Canonical Forms for Threshold Operation, *Tech. Rept.* TR64–5–BF, Jan. 31, 1964 (Litton Systems, Inc.), submitted to *JASA*, 1964.
19. Kelly, E. J., I. S. Reed, and W. L. Root: The Detection of Radar Echoes in Noise: I, *J. Soc. Ind. Appl. Math.* **8**(2):309–341 (1960); in particular, *ibid.*, **8**(3):481–507 (1960).
20. Middleton, D.: On Singular and Non-singular Optimum (Bayes) Tests for the Detection of Normal Stochastic Signals in Normal Noise, *IRE, Trans. Inform. Theory*, **IT-7**:105–113 (1961); in particular, *ibid.*, **IT-8**:385–387 (1962).
21. Wainstein, L. A., and V. D. Zubakov: "Extraction of Signals from Noise," appendix III, trans. by R. A. Silverman, Prentice-Hall, Inc., Englewood Cliffs, N.J., 1962.
22. M. Rosenblatt (ed.): "Time Series Analysis," John Wiley & Sons, Inc., New York, 1963. (See especially chaps. 19–22.)
23. Root, W. L.: "Singular Gaussian Measures in Detection Theory," in M. Rosenblatt (ed.): "Time Series Analysis," John Wiley & Sons, Inc., New York, 1963, chap. 20.
24. Yaglom, A. M.: "On the Equivalence and Perpendicularity of Two Gaussian Probability Measures in Function Space," in M. Rosenblatt (ed.): "Time Series Analysis," John Wiley & Sons, Inc., New York, 1963, chap. 22.
25. Grettenberg, T. L.: Signal Selection in Communication and Radar Systems, *IEEE, Trans. Inform. Theory*, **IT-9**:265 (1963), and references therein.
26. Marcus, M. B., and P. Swerling: Sequential Detection in Radar with Multiple Resolution Elements, *IRE, Trans. Inform. Theory*, **IT-6**:237 (1962).
27. Sebesteyn, G. S.: "Decision-making Processes in Pattern Recognition," The Macmillan Company, New York, 1962.
28. Pugachev, V. S.: "Theory of Random Functions and Their Application to Automatic Control Problems," 3d ed., Fismatgiz., Moscow-Leningrad, 1962.
29. Bellman, R.: "Adaptive Control Processes," Princeton University Press, Princeton, N.J., 1961.
30. Schweppe, F. C.: Optimization of Signals, *Mass. Inst. Technol. Res. Lab. Electron. Tech. Rept.* 1964-4, Jan. 16, 1964.
31. Bello, P.: Characterization of Randomly Time-variant Linear Channels, *IEEE, Trans. Commun. Systems*, **CS-11**:360 (1963).
32. Petersen, D. P., and D. Middleton: Linear Interpolation, Extrapolation, and Prediction of Random Space-Time Fields with a Limited Domain of Measurement, *IEEE, Trans. Inform. Theory*, **IT-11**, Jan., 1965.

Bibliography

Besides the books and papers cited in Chaps. 1 to 5, and primarily in addition and subsequent to the references contained in the author's "Introduction to Statistical Communication Theory" (see the Preface of the present monograph), the following short list of books, both introductory and advanced, is called to the reader's attention.

1. Abramson, N.: "Information Theory and Coding," McGraw-Hill Book Company, New York, 1963.
2. Bennett, W. R.: "Electrical Noise," McGraw-Hill Book Company, New York, 1960.
3. Brillouin, L.: "Science and Information Theory," 2d ed., Academic Press Inc., New York, 1956.
4. Harman, W. W.: "Principles of the Statistical Theory of Communication," McGraw-Hill Book Company, New York (1963).
5. Kotel'nikov, V. A.: "The Theory of Optimum Noise Immunity," trans. by R. A. Silverman, McGraw-Hill Book Company, New York, 1960.
6. Lee, Y. W.: "Statistical Theory of Communication," John Wiley & Sons, Inc., New York, 1960.

7. O'Neill, E. L.: "Introduction to Statistical Optics," Addison-Wesley Publishing Company, Inc., Reading, Mass., 1963.
8. Parzen, E.: "Stochastic Processes," Holden-Day, San Francisco, Calif., 1962.
9. Skolnik, M. I.: "Introduction to Radar Systems," McGraw-Hill Book Company, New York, 1962.
10. Tatarski, V. I.: "Wave Propagation in a Turbulent Medium," trans. by R. A. Silverman, McGraw-Hill Book Company, New York, 1961.
11. Wolfowitz, J.: "The Coding Theorems of Information Theory," Prentice-Hall, Inc., Englewood, N.J. and Springer-Verlag OHG, Berlin, 1961.
12. Yaglom, A. M.: "An Introduction to the Theory of Stationary Random Functions," trans. by R. A. Silverman, Prentice-Hall, Inc., Englewood Cliffs, N.J., 1962.
13. Zadeh, L. A., and C. A. Desoer: "Linear System Theory," McGraw-Hill Book Company, New York, 1963.
14. Beran, M. J., and G. P. Parrent, Jr.: "The Theory of Partial Coherence," Prentice-Hall, Inc., Englewood Cliffs, N.J., 1964.
15. Blanc-LaPierre, A.: "Modèles statistiques pour l'étude de phénomènes de fluctuations," Masson et Cie, Paris, 1963.

Appendix

The distribution density for the background noise, which is fundamental to most applications, is the multivariate gaussian density[1]

$$W_n(\mathbf{V})_N = \frac{e^{-\frac{1}{2}\tilde{\mathbf{v}}\mathbf{k}_N^{-1}\mathbf{v}}}{(2\pi)^{n/2}(\det \mathbf{k}_N)^{\frac{1}{2}}} \qquad \text{(A.1)}$$

where $\mathbf{v}$ $(= \mathbf{n})$ is the normalized n-component (column) vector $\mathbf{v} = \mathbf{V}/\sqrt{\psi} = (\mathbf{N}/\sqrt{\psi}) = [v(t_1), \ldots, v(t_n)]$, consisting of the n samples $v(t_1), \ldots, v(t_n)$ of $V(t)$ taken on the observation interval $(0,T)$; cf. Fig. 1.3; $\mathbf{k}_N$ is the $(n \times n)$ normalized covariance matrix $\mathbf{k}_N = \tilde{\mathbf{k}}_N = \mathbf{K}_N/\psi = [\overline{N(t_j)N(t_k)}]/\overline{N^2}$, with $\bar{N} = 0$ without serious loss of generality, and det $\mathbf{k}_N$ is the determinant of $\mathbf{k}_N$. The exponent of Eq. (A.1) is the positive definite quadratic form

$$\tilde{\mathbf{v}}\mathbf{k}_N^{-1}\mathbf{v} = \sum_{jk}^{n} v_j(k_N^{-1})_{jk}v_k \qquad (>0) \qquad \text{(A.2)}$$

where it is assumed that $\mathbf{k}_N$ is nonsingular, so that the inverse, $\mathbf{k}_N^{-1}$, exists; the ($\sim$) denotes the transposed vector (or matrix). When signal and noise are combined in some fashion [$V = S \otimes N$], the conditional d.d. of $\mathbf{V}$ becomes

$$F_n(\mathbf{V}|\mathbf{S}) = W_n[\mathbf{N}(\mathbf{V},\mathbf{S})]_N \left| \frac{\partial \mathbf{N}}{\partial \mathbf{V}} \right| = W_n(\mathbf{V} - \mathbf{S})_N \qquad \text{(A.3)}$$

this last in the usual situations of additive noise. Since $\mathbf{v} = a_0\mathbf{s} + \mathbf{n}$ [cf. Eq. (2.42)] for additive, normalized signal and noise, we have at once from this in Eqs. (A.1) and (A.3)

$$F_n(\mathbf{V}|\mathbf{S}) = \frac{e^{-\frac{1}{2}(\tilde{\mathbf{v}} - a_0\tilde{\mathbf{s}})\mathbf{k}_N^{-1}(\mathbf{v} - a_0\mathbf{s})}}{(2\pi)^{n/2}(\det \mathbf{k}_N)^{\frac{1}{2}}} \qquad \text{(A.4)}$$

which is the desired relation (2.41).

With continuous sampling on the observation interval $(0,T)$, we obtain formally the quadratic functionals

$$\begin{aligned} (\Phi_T)_s &= \lim_{n\to\infty} \Phi_s = \lim_{n\to\infty} \tilde{\mathbf{s}}\mathbf{k}_N^{-1}\mathbf{s} \\ (\Phi_T)_v &= \lim_{n\to\infty} \Phi_v = \lim_{n\to\infty} \tilde{\mathbf{v}}\mathbf{k}_N^{-1}\mathbf{s} \end{aligned} \qquad \text{(A.5)}$$

By the techniques of sec. 19.4-2 in Ref. 1, these can be expressed as

$$(\Phi_T)_s = \psi \int_{0-}^{T+} s(t - \epsilon_0, \boldsymbol{\theta}_0) X_T(t;\epsilon_0,\boldsymbol{\theta}_0)\, dt \qquad \text{(A.6a)}$$

$$(\Phi_T)_v = \psi \int_{0-}^{T+} v(t) X_T(t;\epsilon_0,\boldsymbol{\theta}_0)\, dt \qquad \text{(A.6b)}$$

where X_T is the solution of the basic inhomogeneous integral equation

$$\int_{0-}^{T+} K_N(t,u) X_T(u;\epsilon_0,\boldsymbol{\theta}_0)\, du = s(t - \epsilon_0, \boldsymbol{\theta}_0) \qquad 0- < t < T+ \qquad \text{(A.7)}$$

[As before, ϵ_0 is a known signal epoch, and $\boldsymbol{\theta}_0$ represents one or more (known) signal parameters.] The solution X_T of Eq. (A.7) vanishes outside† $(0-,T+)$.

In a similar fashion, when the signal is deterministic *and* narrow-band [cf. (2.56)], so that we can write

$$s(t - \epsilon; \boldsymbol{\theta}_0) = F_s(t;\boldsymbol{\theta}_0) \cos\,[\omega_0(t - \epsilon) - \varphi_s(t;\boldsymbol{\theta}_0)] \qquad \text{(A.8)}$$

we find that the quadratic functions for incoherent reception (Sec. 2.6) that are analogous to $(\Phi_T)_s$ and $(\Phi_T)_v$ above for coherent observation

† Ref. 1, appendix 2, and sec. A.2-4, in particular, for explicit solutions when the kernel $K_N(t,u)$ is rational.

(Sec. 2.5) are respectively B_T and $\Psi_0(v)_T(=\Psi_0)$; cf. Eqs. (2.58*a*) and (2.58*b*),† e.g.,

$$
\begin{aligned}
B_T &= \lim_{n\to\infty} B_n = \lim_{n\to\infty} \langle \tilde{\mathbf{s}}\mathbf{k}_N^{-1}\mathbf{s}\rangle_\epsilon \\
&= \frac{\psi}{2}\int_{-\infty}^{\infty} F_s(t;\boldsymbol{\theta}_0)\{X_T(t;\boldsymbol{\theta}_0)_0 \cos[\omega_0 t - \varphi_s(t;\boldsymbol{\theta}_0)] \\
&\qquad + Y_T(t;\boldsymbol{\theta}_0)_0 \sin[\omega_0 t - \varphi_s(t;\boldsymbol{\theta}_0)]\}\, dt \qquad \text{(A.9a)}
\end{aligned}
$$

and

$$
\begin{aligned}
\Psi_0(v)_T &= \lim_{n\to\infty} \Psi_0(\mathbf{v})_n = \lim_{n\to\infty} \tilde{\mathbf{v}}\langle \mathbf{k}_N^{-1}\mathbf{k}_S\mathbf{k}_N^{-1}\rangle_\epsilon \mathbf{v} \\
&= \psi^2 \iint_{-\infty}^{\infty} v(t) D_T(t,u;\boldsymbol{\theta}_0)_0 v(u)\, dt\, du \qquad \text{(A.9b)}
\end{aligned}
$$

with

$$
\begin{aligned}
D_T &= X_T(t;\boldsymbol{\theta}_0)_0 X_T(u;\boldsymbol{\theta}_0)_0 + Y_T(t;\boldsymbol{\theta}_0)_0 Y_T(u;\boldsymbol{\theta}_0)_0 \qquad 0- < t,\ u < T+ \\
&= 0 \qquad \text{elsewhere.} \qquad \text{(A.9c)}
\end{aligned}
$$

The X_{0T}, Y_{0T} here are analogous to Eq. (A.7), the solutions of the *pair* of basic inhomogeneous integral equations

$$
\int_{0-}^{T+} K_N(t,u) \begin{Bmatrix} X_T(u;\boldsymbol{\theta}_0)_0 \\ Y_T(u;\boldsymbol{\theta}_0)_0 \end{Bmatrix} du = \begin{Bmatrix} F_s \cos(\omega_0 t - \varphi_s) \\ F_s \sin(\omega_0 t - \varphi_s) \end{Bmatrix} \qquad \text{(A.10)}
$$

Both X_{0T} and Y_{0T} vanish outside the observation period $(0-,T+)$. With a complex filter structure

$$
Z_T(t;\boldsymbol{\theta}_0)_0 \equiv X_T(t;\boldsymbol{\theta}_0)_0 + iY_T(t;\boldsymbol{\theta}_0)_0 \qquad \text{(A.11)}
$$

we can express the above more compactly as

$$
B_T = \frac{\psi}{2}\,\mathrm{Re}\int_{-\infty}^{\infty} F_s(t;\boldsymbol{\theta}_0) Z_T(t;\boldsymbol{\theta}_0)_0^* e^{i\omega_0 t - i\varphi_s(t;\boldsymbol{\theta}_0)}\, dt \qquad \text{(A.12a)}
$$

$$
\Psi_0 = \left|\sqrt{\psi}\int_{-\infty}^{\infty} V(t) Z_T(t;\boldsymbol{\theta}_0)_0\, dt\right|^2 \qquad Z_T = 0 \text{ outside } (0,T) \qquad \text{(A.12b)}
$$

where (*) denotes the complex conjugate. The pair of integral equations (A.10) are now combined into a single relation:

$$
\int_{0-}^{T+} K_N(t,u) Z_T(u;\boldsymbol{\theta}_0)_0\, du = F_s(t;\boldsymbol{\theta}_0) e^{i\omega_0 t - i\varphi_s} \qquad \text{(A.13)}
$$

for $(0- < t < T+)$. Here Z_{0T}, like X_{0T}, Y_{0T}, and X_T above, can be interpreted as a (Bayes) matched filter (of the second kind, type 3); cf. Table 4.1.

† Ref. 1, sec. 20.2-3.

With white (normal) noise backgrounds the solutions of the basic integral equations (A.7), (A.10), and (A.13) are found by inspection, since now the noise kernel K_N becomes†

$$K_N(t,u)_{\text{white}} = \frac{W_0}{2}\,\delta(t-u) \tag{A.14}$$

when W_0 is the spectral intensity density, as before.

We have

$$\begin{aligned} X_T &= \frac{2}{W_0}\, s(t-\epsilon_0;\, \boldsymbol{\theta}_0) \\ \begin{Bmatrix} X_{0T} \\ Y_{0T} \end{Bmatrix} &= \frac{2}{W_0}\, F_s(t;\boldsymbol{\theta}_0) \begin{Bmatrix} \cos(\omega_0 t - \varphi_s) \\ \sin(\omega_0 t - \varphi_s) \end{Bmatrix} \end{aligned} \tag{A.15}$$

and therefore

$$Z_{0T} = \frac{2}{W_0}\, F_s e^{i(\omega_0 t - \varphi_s)} \qquad 0 \le t \le T \tag{A.15a}$$

with $X_T = Z_{0T} = \ldots = 0$ outside $(0,T)$, of course. From these follow Eqs. (2.52), (2.53), and (2.68) to (2.71).

We remark that when $\boldsymbol{\theta}_0$ is not known but is treated as a (set of) random parameters, Φ_s, $(\Phi_T)_s$, etc., are replaced by $\Phi_{\bar{s}}$, $(\Phi_T)_{\bar{s}}$, etc.; we must include the pertinent statistical averages over $s(t;\boldsymbol{\theta}_0)$. Similarly, in the incoherent cases B_T and Ψ_0 are modified to

$$B_T = \frac{\psi}{2}\,\mathrm{Re} \int_{-\infty}^{\infty} \langle F_s(t;\boldsymbol{\theta}) Z_T(t;\boldsymbol{\theta})_0 e^{i\omega_0 t - i\varphi_s} \rangle_{\boldsymbol{\theta}}\, dt \tag{A.16a}$$

$$\begin{aligned} \Psi_0 &= \psi \left\langle \left| \int_{-\infty}^{\infty} V(t) Z_T(t;\boldsymbol{\theta})_0\, dt \right|^2 \right\rangle_{\boldsymbol{\theta}} \\ &= \psi \iint_{-\infty}^{\infty} V(t) \langle Z_T(t;\boldsymbol{\theta})_0 Z_T(u;\boldsymbol{\theta})_0^* \rangle_{\boldsymbol{\theta}} V(u)\, dt\, du \end{aligned} \tag{A.16b}$$

Now, of course, Z_{0T} is no longer a matched filter form. It is with $\langle ZZ^* \rangle_{\boldsymbol{\theta}} \equiv G_0(t,u)$ that we must deal [cf. Eqs. (4.41)], resolving it instead into type 1 or 2 Bayes matched filters (of the second kind), in order to provide a structural interpretation of the data functional Ψ_0; cf. Sec. 4.3 and Figs. 4.3 and 4.4.

Finally, in the case of the incoherent detection process considered above, the error probabilities are expressible as Q functions.[2] These

† Ref. 1, sec. 3.2-3.

have the following important properties:

$$Q(\alpha;\beta) \equiv \int_\beta^\infty e^{-\alpha^2/2-x^2/2} x I_0(\alpha x)\, dx \qquad \beta \geq 0;\ \alpha^2 > 0 \quad \text{(A.17)}$$

with

$$Q(\alpha;0) = 1 \qquad Q(0;\beta) = e^{-\beta^2/2} \qquad Q(\alpha;\infty) = 0 \quad \text{(A.17}a\text{)}$$

Other useful relations are

$$Q(\alpha;\beta) = e^{-(\alpha^2+\beta^2)/2} \sum_{n=0}^{\infty} (\alpha/\beta)^n I_n(\alpha\beta) \qquad 0 \leq \alpha < \beta$$

$$= 1 - e^{-(\alpha^2+\beta^2)/2} \sum_{n=0}^{\infty} (\beta/\alpha)^n I_n(\alpha\beta) \qquad 0 \leq \beta < \alpha \quad \text{(A.18)}$$

and

$$Q(\alpha;\beta) \simeq \tfrac{1}{2}\left[1 - \Theta\left(\frac{\beta-\alpha}{\sqrt{2}}\right)\right][1 + \frac{1}{8\alpha^2} + O(\alpha^{-4})] \qquad \alpha \gg 1$$

$$\text{all } \beta \geq 0 \quad \text{(A.19)}$$

An interesting Fourier transform relation is[3]

$$\mathfrak{F}\left\{\frac{e^{\pm i\xi a_2^2/4(1\mp i\xi a_2)}}{(1 \mp i\xi a_2)(1 \pm i\xi a_1)}\right\} = \frac{e^{-\frac{a_2^2}{4(a_1+a_2)} \pm z/a_1}}{a_1 + a_2}$$

$$\cdot \begin{cases} Q\left(\sqrt{\dfrac{a_1 a_2}{2(a_1+a_2)}};\ \sqrt{\dfrac{2(\pm z)(a_1+a_2)}{a_1+a_2}}\right) & z \geq 0\ (+) \\ & z \leq 0\ (-) \\ 1 \qquad z \leq 0\ (+) \\ \qquad z \geq 0\ (-) \end{cases} \quad \text{(A.20)}$$

where a_1, $a_2 \geq 0$ and are real.

References

1. Middleton, D.: "An Introduction to Statistical Communication Theory," sec. 7.3, McGraw-Hill Book Company, New York, 1960.
2. Marcum, J. I.: Tables of Q-Functions, *RAND Corp.* RM-339; *ASTIA Doc.* AD-116551, Jan. 1, 1950.
3. Middleton, D.: Canonical Forms for Error Probabilities in Binary Bayes Detection, *Air Force Cambridge Res. Lab. Rept.* AFCRL-63-561, December, 1963.

Glossary of Principal Symbols

A_0	peak signal amplitude
a_0^2, $\overline{a_{0u}^2}$, $\overline{a_{0R}^2}$	input signal-to-noise (power) ratios
a_0^*, A_0^*	optimum estimators of amplitude
α	type 1 error probability
$\hat{B}_n$, B_T	biases
β, $\beta_1^{(0)}$, $\beta_0^{(1)}$, $\beta_0^{(1)*}$, $\beta_1^{(0)*}$	error probabilities
$C_1^{(0)}$, $C_0^{(1)}$, $C_1^{(1)}$, $C_0^{(0)}$	constant costs
c.f.	characteristic function
$C(\mathbf{S},\gamma)$	cost function
$D_T(t,u)$, $D_T(t,u)_0$	kernels of a quadratic form
d.d.	distribution density
δ, δ^*	decision rules
E_s, $\bar{E}_s$	signal energy
$\boldsymbol{E}$, $\boldsymbol{E}_{v\|s}$, etc.	expectation operators
ϵ, ϵ_0	signal epochs
$F(i\xi\|H)$	characteristic function

F_s	envelope of narrow-band signal
$\mathfrak{F}$	Fourier functions
$\mathfrak{F}_1, \mathfrak{F}_2$	cost functions
$F_n(\mathbf{V}\|\mathbf{S})$	conditional d.d. of **V**, given **S**.
$\mathbf{G}_0, G^{(1)}, G^{(2)}$	kernels of quadratic forms
Γ	data space
$\gamma; \boldsymbol{\gamma}, \boldsymbol{\gamma}_\sigma$	decisions; estimators
$H_{0,1}$	hypotheses
$h, h_M, \hat{h}, H_c(t,\tau)$	weighting function of filters
$I_0(x), I_1(x)$	modified Bessel function of first kind, 0th and 1st orders
$\mathbf{K}_N, K_N$	noise covariance matrix and covariance function
$\mathbf{k}_N, k_N$	normalized covariance matrix and covariance function of noise background
$\mathcal{K}, \mathcal{K}', K_T$	detection thresholds
Λ_n, Λ_T	likelihood ratio, likelihood functional
λ	fraction of the true value of a parameter under interval estimation
m	sample size (in sequential sampling)
μ	ratio of a priori probabilities
$N(t), \mathbf{N}$	noise wave; noise vector
n	sample size
$\mathbf{n}$	normalized noise vector
$\Omega, \Omega_0, \Omega_1$	portions of signal space
ω, ω_0	angular frequencies
$P, p(\ \ )$	probabilities
$p_1, p_2, (p,q)$	a priori probabilities
Φ_n	quadratic form
$\Phi_s, (\Phi_T)_s$	2 times signal processing gain
$\Phi_v, (\Phi_T)_v$	data functionals
φ_s	signal phase
Ψ_0, Ψ_n, Ψ_T	quadratic forms
ψ	average noise intensity
$Q(\alpha,\beta)$	Q function
$\mathbf{Q}, \mathbf{Q}_c$	weighting functions of a discrete filter
R	average risk
R^*	Bayes risk
$\mathcal{R}_0$	residual risk

ρ, ρ_c	weighting functions
$\boldsymbol{\varrho}$	normalized signal covariance
$\mathbf{S}$, $S(t)$	signals (discrete and continuous)
$S(f)$	amplitude spectrum of a signal
$\mathbf{s}$, $s(t)$	normalized signals (discrete and continuous)
σ^2, σ_0^2, σ_R^2	output signal-to-noise (power) ratios
$\sigma(S)$, $\sigma(\theta)$	a priori d.d.'s
T	data-acquisition period or observational interval
$\boldsymbol{T}_R^{(N)}$, $\boldsymbol{T}_M^{(N)}$, $\boldsymbol{T}_T^{(N)}$	system operators or transformations
Θ, Θ^{-1}	error function and its inverse
$\boldsymbol{\theta}$, $\boldsymbol{\theta}_0$	a set of signal parameters
θ	a measure of input signal-to-noise ratio; a signal parameter
$\mathbf{V}$, $V(t)$	received input data (discrete and continuous)
$\mathbf{v}$, $v(t)$	normalized data
W_1, W_n, w_1, w_n	probability densities
W_0	spectral density of white noise
X_T, X_{T0}	solution of a basic integral equation
x, $\hat{x}$, x_0	optimum detector or estimator (test statistic)
Y_{T0}	solution of a basic integral equation
y, y_R	optimum detectors
z_0	optimum estimator
Z_T	complex weighting function

Name Index

Subject Index